Building a Successful Family Business Board

A FAMILY———
BUSINESS
———PUBLICATION

Family Business Publications are the combined efforts of the Family Business Consulting Group and Palgrave Macmillan. These books provide useful information on a broad range of topics that concern the family business enterprise, including succession planning, communication, strategy and growth, family leadership, and more. The books are written by experts with combined experiences of over a century in the field of family enterprise and who have consulted with thousands of enterprising families the world over, giving the reader practical, effective, and time-tested insights to everyone involved in a family business.

, founded in 1994, is the leading business consultancy exclusively devoted to helping family enterprises prosper across generations.

Building a Successful Family Business Board

A Guide for Leaders, Directors, and Families

Jennifer M. Pendergast, John L. Ward, and Stephanie Brun de Pontet

BUILDING A SUCCESSFUL FAMILY BUSINESS BOARD

Copyright © Jennifer M. Pendergast, John L. Ward, and Stephanie Brun de Pontet, 2011.

All rights reserved.

First published in 2011 by
PALGRAVE MACMILLAN®
in the United States—a division of St. Martin's Press LLC,
175 Fifth Avenue, New York, NY 10010.

Where this book is distributed in the UK, Europe and the rest of the world, this is by Palgrave Macmillan, a division of Macmillan Publishers Limited, registered in England, company number 785998, of Houndmills, Basingstoke, Hampshire RG21 6XS.

Palgrave Macmillan is the global academic imprint of the above companies and has companies and representatives throughout the world.

Palgrave® and Macmillan® are registered trademarks in the United States, the United Kingdom, Europe and other countries.

ISBN: 978–0–230–11154–7

Library of Congress Cataloging-in-Publication Data

Pendergast, Jennifer M.
    Building a successful family business board : a guide for leaders, directors, and families / by Jennifer M. Pendergast, John L. Ward, and Stephanie Brun de Pontet.
        p. cm. — (A Family business publication)
    Includes bibliographical references and index.
    ISBN 978–0–230–11154–7
    1. Family-owned business enterprises—Management. 2. Family corporations—Management. 3. Boards of directors. I. Ward, John L., 1945– II. De Pontet, Stephanie Brun. III. Title.

HD62.25.P46 2011
658.4'22—dc22   2010030268

A catalogue record of the book is available from the British Library.

Design by Newgen Imaging Systems (P) Ltd., Chennai, India.

First edition: February 2011

10 9 8 7 6 5 4 3 2 1

Printed in the United States of America.

Contents

Foreword   vii

1   Independent Boards of Directors and
    Family Business: Introduction to
    a Powerful Alliance   1

2   Truth and Myths about
    Boards: Meeting the Challenge   9

3   The Role of the Board in the Family Business   25

4   The Special Value of Independent
    Directors to the Family Business   35

5   The Vital Role of the Board in
    Family Business Continuity Planning   53

6   Designing the Board   67

7   Finding and Selecting Directors   89

8   Managing the Board   117

9   Making the Most of Your Board   145

10 Linking Family and Business
    Governance in Later Generations   165

11 How You Can Contribute As a Director   189

12 Our Call to Action   211

Appendix 1	Example Board Prospectus	217
Appendix 2	Committee Responsibilities	222
Appendix 3	Family Director Qualifications and Nominating Process	227
Appendix 4	Introductory Letter to Accompany Prospectus	231
Appendix 5	Rating Sheet to Aid in Director Selection Meeting	232
Appendix 6	Board of Directors Evaluation	233
Appendix 7	Chairman Job Description	236
Appendix 8	Smith Family Assembly Charter	239
Appendix 9	Summay of Survey Results	249
Bibliography		253
Index		255

Foreword

This book is an updated, revised, and substantially rewritten successor to *Creating Effective Boards for Private Enterprises* (John L. Ward, Jossey-Bass Publishers, 1991). The focus of this new book is different, supported by new survey research and co-written with two talented colleagues in The Family Business Consulting Group.

In the original book, the purpose was to persuade business founders and owner-managers of privately held small and mid-size companies (50 to 500 employees) to establish an "outside board"— a group composed of three or four other business owner-managers to stimulate their strategic thinking, to prepare for succession, and to challenge themselves with increased accountability. I believed then and I believe now that such a board—a voluntary act by a controlling owner-manager—is the best resource possible for leadership and business effectiveness. The original book went on to show the business owner how to form such a board and how to use it to its fullest advantage.

Happily, several thousand copies were sold. While I wish I knew how many did put an "outside board" together, I do know that nearly all that I have met who did so extol its benefits.

A lot has changed over the years. Most compellingly, the study of multigeneration family businesses has blossomed. Twenty years ago there were only a handful of books on family business, very few business schools interested in the subject, and virtually no consulting organizations devoted to family enterprise continuity. That has all changed.

Today, more and more family businesses are owned by larger groups of family members who may, or may not, work in the business. Primogeniture ownership succession is less common. Instead, it is becoming increasingly common for families, especially in the Western Hemisphere, to divide the family's business ownership more equally among a greater number of family members. This trend, of course, raises powerful questions on the roles and responsibilities of family members in governance.

Concurrently, the general topic of corporate governance has grown in importance. From Enron to Parmalat to Lehman Brothers, governance practices have been questioned and interest in developing effective oversight has grown exponentially. As a result of many perceived corporate governance failures in recent years, boards have become more vigilant overseers of management behavior and corporate performance.

At the same time, legislation has been enacted with new proposals on the table every year to strengthen oversight, primarily of public companies. Many business schools, including my own (Kellogg Business School at Northwestern University), have created intense training and coursework to understand the proper functions of governance, and to prepare people for directorships and chairmanships.

While the topic of governance is certainly in the limelight, this heightened focus sometimes generates "noise" that leads to the too-frequent loss of two important truths. First, while high-profile cases have raised concerns about lack of appropriate oversight, most companies have sound ethics and an unselfish long-term view. Certainly that is especially true for businesses owned by families, for whom values-driven culture and perpetuity of ownership are hallmarks.

Second, we are keen to promote in this book the concept that effective boards are a particularly great value-added resource for success and succession, not just a protector of stakeholder interests. According to our research survey and our working definition, an effective board is one that meets at least three times a year, is well-organized and managed, and includes three or more independent (i.e., "outside") directors.

Since our previous book was published, we have grown to appreciate even more the special benefits of an effective board to businesses owned by later generation families. In addition, we know these boards frequently (in 60 percent of cases) will include nonemployed family owners, and specific guidance is needed on how to best integrate this resource into an effective board.

So, in *Building a Successful Family Business Board*, we not only shift our focus to *family* enterprises, but also to older and larger families and businesses where the role of family on the board is also important, as well as to the essential role of independent directors. From our consultations with such families, we know how vital and sensitive the processes of selecting family and independent directors are; we also know how essential and often under-considered is the process of preparing directors for service on the family business board—both independent and family directors. We devote several chapters to these topics. We incorporate from our survey the experiences of more than 350 family businesses. (We are particularly appreciative to the Young Presidents Organization/World Presidents Organization for their invaluable participation in the survey.)

Also new to this book is the participation of co-authors, both colleagues who are independent authorities on family business governance. Jennifer Pendergast holds a PhD in corporate governance, and is a long-time consultant to business families, and the head of the governance practice for The Family Business Consulting Group. In that role she has likely assembled more boards for more family businesses than anyone, anywhere. Jennifer is our lead author.

Stephanie Brun de Pontet holds a PhD in psychology, is an experienced and published consultant, and also a member of The Family Business Consulting Group, with particular interest in generational successions and developing the next generation for governance roles. Stephanie also led our research studies.

Jennifer and Stephanie both reshaped this book substantially. And, in order to collate our three voices and perspectives, we benefited greatly from the editing assistance of Jeff Wuorio.

In all our thinking, we acknowledge and genuinely appreciate the special knowledge of our colleagues in The Family Business Consulting Group, Inc. Collectively they have brought to us 200 man-years of devoted family business consulting experience and insight from more than 500 family business boards. In addition, we thank the families who graciously offered to share the stories of how they developedand use their boards, to serve as role models for their family-business peers.

As in the first book, we hope to persuade you that an effective board is your most valuable resource. We hope we have provided a very practical and comprehensive guide to establishing a board and maximizing its effectiveness. New is our particular focus on family businesses—large as well as smaller, family business boardrooms, and family members as directors.

Please share your comments, questions and experiences with us and your fellow readers at http://familybusiness consultinggroup.com.

John L. Ward
Chicago, Illinois

Independent Boards of Directors and Family Business: Introduction to a Powerful Alliance

When Robert Rodale, second-generation CEO of Rodale, Inc., died in a car accident, his wife, Ardath, was thrust into the leadership role. Current CEO and third-generation member Maria Rodale says, "When my father was alive, he never would have used a board. At the moment he died, we put a board in place—to educate our generation, give us insights into the business, and support our mother."

Rodale's first board was comprised of Ardath, Maria and her siblings, and several nonfamily managers. Maria continues: "As we got our sea legs, our generation started to get more involved and active and become true board members." The board faced its first challenge when the most senior nonfamily manager announced he would retire in two years. "We were worried his departure would be very disruptive. As family members, we came together to address the succession." They decided to do a full, widespread search for the next CEO. As a result, two internal candidates for successor left the company, and Rodale hired a new nonfamily CEO from the outside. "At that point, we also decided that adding independent directors would be crucial to our success going forward. The presence of independent, objective oversight for our new CEO gave us confidence in transitioning to non-family leadership."

Challenges such as the one faced by Rodale—and the integral role played by the company's board of directors—are nothing new to businesses, particularly family-owned businesses. They illustrate an essential, yet powerful, truth—that an active, independent board of directors is a most valuable tool for family businesses of all types. There is substantial value added when the objectivity and experience of independent directors combines with the legacy and commitment of family ownership.

The Family Business Boards Study conducted for this book bears this out in numerous ways. We will be referencing findings and the specific demographics of our study throughout the book (summary in appendix 9). A few central results are worth noting at the outset of our discussion, including:

- An active board is perceived as a very valuable tool for managing complexity in a family business.
- Boards with independent directors are viewed as being more effective than boards comprised only of family members.
- Nonemployed family directors play a pivotal role on family business boards and should receive formal preparation to fulfill this role.
- Despite the perceived value of an active board, particularly one with independent directors, boards are still underused by most family businesses.

These and other findings further substantiate the value of an effective board for family businesses and the need for a better understanding of how to build and use boards. To be clear on meaning at the outset, when we use the words "active board," we refer to a board that meets three or more times per year. Further, when we refer to "independent directors," we mean individuals with no other ties to the business or family (not employees, not advisors, not shareholders) who serve on the board. Finally, when we use the term "independent board" this indicates a board with meaningful independent representation, preferably three or more independent directors, the number we believe is required to have a meaningful impact on governance.

Although all companies are required by law to appoint an official board of directors—at least on paper—owners decide whether they wish to create an effective board that adds value to the business.

Board Insight

The central theme of this book is that an active board comprised of a mix of independent and owner directors is an invaluable tool for any business, regardless of ownership structure or size.

A well-constructed, energetic and involved board of directors can prove essential to family-owned businesses of all types, providing direction, feedback and oversight on a variety of issues and challenges. To better understand how family businesses actually use their boards, we have conducted extensive research to break down the structure, use, and value of family business boards, particularly examining how these indicators vary based upon the maturity and complexity of the family business system.

Importance of Boards in a Family Business

By law, a board must be named to fulfill the responsibilities of selecting and removing corporate officers, setting officer compensation and declaring dividends. Most functioning boards take on a more expansive role, reviewing and approving budgets, strategic plans, and policies; overseeing the audit process, and approving significant capital expenditures.

While these board responsibilities are common to all types of businesses, the board of directors of a family business can contribute in unique ways. For instance, independent directors can play a valuable role in ensuring all shareholders are equally represented, setting compensation for family members in management, reviewing the performance of family members in the business, and ensuring that family dynamics do not create conflict in business decision making. By emphasizing professionalism and objectivity, a strong, independent board of directors can help keep family issues and business issues as separate as possible. A 2005 study of family businesses throughout the United Kingdom by the banking concern Coutts found that an independent board of directors decreased the impact of emotions in the family business boardrooms.

The leadership-succession process is one where the board of a family-owned business can play a crucial role. Due to the relationships and emotions involved in family business, succession is often a difficult task. A 2007–08 survey of family businesses by Price Waterhouse Coopers bears this out. One-quarter of the family businesses included in the study were due to change hands within the next five years, yet roughly half the companies that participated in the study had no succession plan in place. A board with independent directors, serving as an objective steward, can oversee the development of a succession plan that makes sense for the business and the family.

Beyond succession planning, a board can help the family business focus on long-term planning and goal setting. The 2007 Laird Norton Tyee Family Business Survey identified a lack of formal planning. Families have the opportunity to think in the long term because they are often committed to a broad family legacy and willing to invest capital with a longer time horizon. Making the most of this potential strategic advantage requires the presence of a long-term plan for the business. The board can help in ensuring that a viable plan is in place.

When is a Board Useful?

Some readers may feel their business is not big enough to leverage the benefits of an active board. In our experience, a board can help almost any family-owned firm that seeks continuity.

Ideally, the board should be in place before the company reaches major—and sometimes predictable—transitions. For instance, a company often hits an "entrepreneurial plateau" when the business outstrips the owner's—or owners'—ability to run it alone. At this point, the energy and expertise of board members are often needed to take the business to the next level. This expertise may include implementing systems or processes to ensure consistency in the business, including budgeting, strategic planning, or performance evaluation and management. These changes to the business may be very challenging for the owner to accept, which underscores why a board needs to be very highly respected by the leader in order to successfully encourage these significant changes that will enable the business to grow to the next level.

In addition to business growth, growth of the family and of the ownership group can also make the role of a board that much more critical. Larger ownership groups make decision making more complicated, requiring a more formal decision making structure and clear delineation of roles among owners, management, and board. The board provides a channel for ownership involvement and concerns, and it facilitates the separation of ownership and management issues. As this separation of ownership and management becomes increasingly complex with a growing ownership group, independent directors are an increasingly crucial part of the mix to make a board effective. In fact, our research establishes that the larger the business and the larger the ownership group the more likely a business is to have independent directors.

Throughout the following chapters, we will make the case for developing a strong, involved board of directors that leverages the skills of independent directors. By focusing on the unique issues, challenges, and opportunities present in family enterprises—and on the role the board plays in addressing them—we will show how a board can be a valuable resource for companies of any size, age, or ownership structure. We will also address the crucial role that qualified, prepared family representation plays on the board. Finally, we will provide detailed advice on how to select board members, both family and independents, and use a board effectively to get the most value for your business and family.

In particular, individual chapters address the following issues:

- In chapter 2, we look at various truths and misinformation that can surround a family business board, and we outline the ways a board can contribute.
- Chapter 3 describes the special value independent directors can bring to a family-owned business board, including succession planning, mentoring of family members, ensuring appropriate compensation levels, and providing strategic perspective from other businesses and industries.
- Chapter 4 begins to go into detail regarding the role of an independent board and how it functions best.
- Chapter 5 details how an independent board can help direct the various sorts of planning necessary for a business to grow and undergo smooth changes in leadership.
- In chapter 6, we look at where to begin in setting up the board—deciding the appropriate mix of owner, management, and independent directors; determining the qualifications and characteristics of independent board members; and developing a board prospectus. This chapter also addresses the practical issues of how many meetings to hold and how to structure them; how to compensate directors; how to create meeting agendas; and how to make the best choice for board chair.
- Chapter 7 shows how to identify and select board members—roles for family and management in the search and nomination processes; determining which owners will sit on the board; how to approach candidates; and what to do if an improper choice is made.
- Chapter 8 addresses strategies for managing the board in and out of meetings—determining what issues are discussed at board meetings; use of the board secretary

and board minutes; and the importance of ongoing evaluation of a board's involvement and performance.

- Chapter 9 covers the varied roles a board can play when working with a family business, including mentoring, development of business vision and goals, and making certain that shareholder opinion is considered.
- Chapter 10 discusses how a board that includes independent directors can help address issues and challenges faced by older, more complex family businesses in the second generation and beyond.
- Chapter 11 is targeted to the directors of family enterprises, helping them determine how they can add most value to the enterprise by asking the right questions, supporting the CEO and helping draw a line between family issues and business issues. This chapter also helps director candidates determine if a position is appropriate for them.
- Chapter 12 is our "Call to Action," summarizing our perspective on the value and contributions of an active, independent board.
- Finally, the appendices provide examples of specific documents family businesses use to develop and manage their boards.

Examination of these and other issues is augmented by profiles of real life family businesses and their boards of directors. These profiles highlight how boards have supported family enterprises in a variety of ways, from goal setting to problem solving. They serve as vivid and provocative examples of the value a carefully constructed and active board of directors can bring to family businesses of all sizes and levels of complexity.

With all the advantages apparent in the presence of a board in a family business, why are so many family businesses unwilling to commit to a strong, effective board? We'll begin considering that question in the next chapter when we discuss the truths and myths that surround a board's makeup and function.

2

Truth and Myths about Boards: Meeting the Challenge

Every business must name a board to meet legal requirements. In our survey, we found that many family businesses stop there. Only 48 percent of respondents have a board that meets more than two times per year. Boards that meet no more than every six months cannot effectively support management during challenges, nor can they provide maximum value to key strategic decisions.

We commend families that have taken the first step to formalizing governance by organizing a board that meets regularly to oversee the business. But it is important to take the next step further, adding independent directors who bring objective oversight and perspective, which significantly enhances board value. Independent directors play a crucial role in holding management and owners accountable and by injecting fresh, unique perspectives into strategic decision making. They bring a level of objectivity free from familial relationships or history with the company.

While data and experience support the value of independent directors, our survey shows that only 25 percent of companies with active boards (those that met three or more times per year) had two or more independent directors on their boards, and 21 percent had three or more independent directors. Even for companies of sales greater than $100 million, only 58 percent had active boards and only 33 percent had three or more independent directors.

In our experience, independent directors are the richest resource available to family-owned companies. So, why do so few companies take advantage of this resource? We have seen that fears about relinquishing control, admitting weakness, or finding directors who truly understand a family's situation limit use of this valuable tool. Examples in this book show that most business owners' fears about independent directors vanish in the light of experience.

For many family businesses in our study, owners and CEOs felt that independent directors brought new ideas, perspectives, insights, or self-confidence. In many cases, independent directors acted as catalysts for important strategic, financial, and succession planning. Almost universally, owners and CEOs reported strategic insights or organizational suggestions that were invaluable.

Independent directors served a critical role as a confidential ally to the chief executive and/or owners in grappling with knotty succession or family issues. Almost unanimously, these owners reported that independent directors have improved the quality of decision making at their companies and increased their chances of perpetuating private ownership, should they choose to do so.

Here are two real-life examples:

- One entrepreneur credits his board with helping his specialty baked goods concern develop an upscale image and a brand name for its new line of cookies. While the board members did not name the products or come up with the packaging design, they really pushed management to define the image they were looking for and asked questions that helped management clearly identify their target customers. "You can see the influence of the board here," says the owner, proudly showing off an array of attractive products.
- Another family-held concern says its independent directors correctly refocused top management's attention toward strategy and long-term planning and away

from day-to-day operating details. One director cites a specific board conversation: "Management asked for our input on a decision to invest in new equipment for the plant. The board members asked management their long-term plan for the product categories that would be produced with the new equipment. We had a concern based on some earlier conversations that this product line may be phased out in the next few years." The board encouraged management to identify a three-year plan, including projected product volumes by category to aid in capacity-planning decisions. The board "has really helped us to move the company forward," says one family member.

In our survey, respondents with independent representation on their boards reported a much higher level of board effectiveness than respondents with no independent directors. And reported effectiveness increases with the amount of independent representation.

Type of board	Percent of sample rated board effective
Family board	54 percent
Two or more independents but NOT a majority	83 percent
Majority independents	96 percent

These results mirror earlier research showing that almost 90 percent of the CEOs with at least two independent directors term their boards "useful," "very valuable," or "tremendously valuable" to the company—a far higher level of satisfaction than that expressed by CEOs with boards of only shareholders, family, or top managers.

Resistance to Boards

With research and testimony for family business owners demonstrating that an independent board is a valuable resource for the family-owned business, why are there not more of them? To be fair, business owners' resistance to creating a board is occasionally well-founded. Sometimes unusual tensions among shareholders weigh against it. In one family business, for instance, the 62-year-old CEO and his wife, the company's financial executive, were eager to hand the business over to their daughter, who was working in the company. However, their energy was consumed by struggling to help hold together the daughter's troubled marriage to a man also employed in the business. In this situation, the family needed to resolve some of these internal problems before it could deal effectively with a board.

In other cases, the family leader's own position is too tenuous to involve active outside directors. Perhaps he has constructed a tense truce among shareholders who are continually nipping at his heels. Another potential challenge a board may create is increased family involvement. Especially in situations where a family member has been troublesome or difficult in the past, an active board—where all owners participate alongside independent directors—may provide another platform for the challenging family member to negatively insert himself or herself into the business.

Some family members are not emotionally prepared to deal with a board. Others are not receptive to constructive advice. All of these may be valid reasons to avoid forming an independent board (although we will argue later in the book that the independent board helps address some of these issues.)

More often, though, resistance is rooted in a lack of experience or understanding of the potential benefits of effective directors—advantages that most often outweigh any drawbacks. Let's take a closer look at some of the reasons most often cited by family company leaders for avoiding a board.

"Why Would I Want a Board Like *That*?"

Many business owners' only experience with independent boards is as directors of local banks or charitable or civic organizations. These are often poor examples. Community banks tend to pick directors for the primary purpose of business development, often packing their boards with customers. Directors in this heavily regulated industry also tend to become mired in operations, meeting monthly, or even more frequently, to vote on loan approvals and other operating matters. Similarly, boards of philanthropic or civic organizations are often assembled with political goals in mind, appealing to various constituencies, building alliances, or aiding fundraising efforts. They are often far larger and more bureaucratic than a business board should be. Boards of publicly traded companies are another well-known model. But their board operations are influenced by a fiduciary responsibility to a diverse and far-flung shareholder base and to public company reporting requirements.

While public company boards can function well despite these obstacles, owners of family businesses typically only hear or read in the media about the worst: boards hit by liability lawsuits, boards ousting company leadership, boards under attack by special interest groups, and boards that crumble from infighting.

Yet, family business owners do not need to embrace any of these models—the bank, philanthropic, or conflict-ridden public company boards. An effective family company board can operate much differently.

While it requires some courage to invite active directors into one's business, says one owner, "The more you understand their role, the less intimidating the whole idea is."

Fears and Misconceptions about Boards

With so few good role models, many family businesses harbor a variety of fears about independent directors. Here are a few of the most common ones:

"Why should I give up control of my company?" Many family business owners suspect independent directors will somehow rob them of control of their business. This fear

obscures the fact that *all* directors serve at the pleasure of shareholders. In the family-owned company, owners structure the board to meet their needs. Few issues need come to a vote.

If independent directors are not aligned with owners' vision and goals, directors can be removed as quickly as a shareholders' meeting can be called. (And in a family-owned company, that can be a matter of a few phone calls.) "Let's face it, in a family-held firm, the family holds all the votes," says one family business owner. "If directors kept disagreeing on decisions we felt strongly about, the owners would disband the board, and we'd move on. But, frankly, I don't imagine that ever happening. They respect us, and we'd be fools not to consider their opinion."

Moreover, a power grab is the furthest thing from the mind of a family company director. Most see their role as a sounding board, a guide, a confidential ally, and a resource. And their motivation is usually to offer help when they can and to learn what they can in the process.

As we mentioned earlier, some family businesses believe a board will merely give certain family members greater opportunity to involve themselves in the business—often, not for the better. In many cases, the opposite is true—a professional and qualified board composed in part of independent members may exert a positive influence on family members who may, in the past, have been disruptive, uncooperative, or merely uninvolved.

"They won't respect our values." Many family businesses are concerned that independent directors will not abide by certain traditions and values that are imbued in the business, such as closing on Sundays, loyalty to employees, or even reticence to take on debt. In fact, a qualified board including qualified independent directors will acknowledge the importance of those values and the effect they have had on the family business' success, rather than trying to change them.

"The liability risk is too great." Both experience and research show this fear is overblown for family company boards. And means of alleviating the risks are certainly available, such as shareholder indemnification or director and officer liability insurance. (These issues are treated in detail in chapter 7.)

Another alternative preferred by many family businesses is the naming of outside advisors to an advisory board rather than to a board of directors. The advisory board does not make any final decisions but provides advice and insight. In most cases, an advisory board can be almost as effective as an independent board.

Ultimately, the best defense against legal liability is conscientious and good faith conduct by the directors—a guiding principle routinely embraced by effective board members.

"I don't want to give up any of my privacy." Many entrepreneurs strongly resist sharing financial information, but as a business grows, financial performance data become crucial management tools. Some level of disclosure to top managers becomes necessary to set goals, measure progress, and grow. Owners need not fear disclosure to well-selected independent directors or advisors, as they will know to treat any confidential information of the business or family with the utmost care and respect, just as if it were their own business.

"I don't have any idea whom to choose." Many families have been too busy building the business to develop an extensive network of outside contacts. Many worry that qualified people will not want to serve; some fear making bad choices. Yet, the process can be virtually fail-safe if approached deliberately and thoughtfully. Business owners typically have more resources at hand than they realize to help identify good candidates, and a careful screening can dramatically reduce the risk of making a poor choice.

"I'm not organized enough to deal with a board." Many business leaders have neglected organizational and management skills in favor of growing their companies. But these are not just boardroom skills. As a company and its workforce grow, leadership's ability to articulate ideas and goals becomes increasingly important to the quality of management. Managing a board can reinforce development of these

professional abilities, leading to benefits throughout the growing business.

"Outsiders could never understand my business." No one will ever understand any family business as well as the family and management team. Good independent directors know that. Effective directors are not there to run the business, nor will they try. Directors will develop valuable knowledge of the company in time. And because good boards tend to focus on broad, long-range issues, such as strategy and succession, the directors' diverse experience can greatly enrich the discussion and, therefore, be an asset rather than a liability. Additionally, qualified independent directors help boost the overall professionalism of any family business—for instance, a board can be instrumental in formalizing various policies and procedures, a step that can prove critical should a sudden change in leadership occur due to death or illness.

In particular, directors who come from a family business background may understand more about running such businesses than you might assume, such as the importance of maintaining the core values a family brings to its business. In that sense, they can bring empathy to their responsibility—a firsthand understanding of the issues and challenges a family business can face.

"Independent directors will force me to act more quickly than I want to." Many family businesses fear that raising an issue with an independent board will force them into quick action. Effective boards do not operate this way. The role of an effective family business board is never to force or coerce, but to listen, lend counsel, encourage and support, and raise questions.

"An independent board would be a bureaucratic headache." Meeting legal requirements for board actions is easy when Mom and Dad and the family lawyer or advisor are the only directors. In practice, though, a well-managed, independent board can deal with its legal duties almost as efficiently, sometimes more efficiently if it can reduce family discord and ineffective decision making.

As stated above, there are many misconceptions about boards—but the reality is: Boards help a business move forward.

Ten Benefits of a Board

1. In-house Experience, Expertise, and Empathy. Independent directors can bring a wealth of experience to a business. A board of risk-taking peers—others who already have passed the milestones that lie ahead for your business—can ease the fear of the unknown and help anticipate new challenges. Directors who have come from a family business know first-hand what challenges a family business can face, and they can genuinely empathize with you about the dilemmas these challenges may create for you in your leadership role.

Often, directors bring a network of personal contacts to the business. At least once in most board meetings, directors offer helpful resources: "If you need advice on this, why don't you talk to so-and-so?" At other times, they offer special expertise that may be peripheral to operations but valuable to the overall smooth functioning of the business—suggestions for a disaster-recovery program or employee-safety training, for instance.

2. Self-discipline and Accountability. As much as many family business owners relish autonomy, many find accountability is a crucial tool in helping to preserve it. If a family business is transparent with its goals, the likelihood of achieving them increases. Many of these owners even ask their boards to review their own performance annually against the goals they have set for themselves. Directors can also prove particularly effective in reassuring owners who are not active in the business.

Often, directors help develop the tools family businesses need to set measurable goals and gauge performance against those goals. Many owners say their boards have helped them master financial reporting techniques, including key performance ratios.

A vigilant board brings another, often unforeseen, benefit: organizational accountability. As the discipline encouraged by independent directors trickles down through the company, many family businesses see improvement in performance at all levels of the organization.

3. A Sounding Board. An experienced board can serve as a valuable sounding board. Like most anyone else, family business owners are full of ideas that range from great to mediocre. What many of them lack is a sounding board to help evaluate those ideas—a panel that is knowledgeable and objective and will listen and react honestly, appropriately, and without unintended consequences. In our survey, the value of a sounding board for senior management was often cited by study respondents as an extremely valuable benefit, ranking second only to "giving input on strategic direction" in a list of the benefits of an independent board.

For the founder of a publishing concern, an independent board pointed out the risks of his idea to affiliate with a foreign partner. "It's easy when you're by yourself to get off on a tangent and come up with something you think is a good idea," the founder says. "But the board helped me see the problem: that the amount of capital I would probably get compared with the independence I would have to give up wouldn't be worth it. As a result of one board discussion, I put it out of my head—after messing around with it for years."

In other cases, a board may give the family the confidence they need to charge ahead. "In business, you've always got one foot on the gas and one on the brake," says one CEO. "The directors are the clutch. They let you know which one should take over."

4. Honest, Objective Opinions. A well-chosen board can provide an excellent forum for gleaning honest, objective opinions. Family business owners and senior executives exert little power or influence over good board members. Effective directors have nothing to prove or gain by promoting their own interests; nor are directors' fees enough to make them beholden to the company. As discussed later, the compensation typically paid directors (in a range of $15,000–$40,000 a year for most small to medium-sized private companies) is certainly not enough to sway the opinion of an experienced business owner or executive.

Instead, typically board members seek the satisfaction of associating with other directors, providing help, and learning something in the process. They enjoy bringing thoughtful and objective insight to an important discussion with peers. Family businesses with independent boards recognize this—our survey found that objectivity was a highly valued board attribute.

Seeking advice from family poses particular pitfalls. "I can't tell my wife I'm worried about how my son-in-law is doing in the business," says one family business owner. "She'll just say, 'You'd better keep him working, because he's got three of our grandchildren to support.'"

This comment illustrates the importance of honest and objective feedback with regard to family business-related issues, such as succession, compensation, differences of opinion, and others. An independent board can provide an essential dose of objectivity in situations where emotions and deep feelings can dominate.

5. *Strategic Planning and Counsel.* It is management's role—not the board's—to set strategy. But many family business owners have found independent directors helpful in prompting them to begin strategic planning, in helping with the process, and in monitoring the plan's implementation. Our survey confirms the value of this function because, as noted by respondents, providing input on strategic direction was the leading benefit provided by the board. In addition, once a plan is developed, the board can help oversee implementation.

6. *Insight into Key People.* Many family business owners are eager for help in evaluating key people. The vice president for sales, the chief financial officer, the leading candidate for a pivotal job, and even the corporate lawyer, banker, or accountant—all are candidates for formal or informal meetings with the board. This interaction gives directors an opportunity to offer candid reactions that can help family

business leaders make important personnel and management decisions. These insights become critically important when evaluating next generation members for leadership positions or investigating the possibility of bringing in non-family leadership for the first time.

Sometimes, directors provide the support needed to dismiss a chief financial officer or manufacturing manager who is performing poorly. In other cases, the board affirms the family business's choice for an important post. Often, directors help set up management development and evaluation systems that provide greater control over employee performance.

Directors can also help evaluate providers of professional services, such as accountants, attorneys, and bankers. These relationships do not lend themselves to shopping around, and directors can help spot inferior performance or can suggest alternatives.

A board can also help family businesses identify and address various "blind spots." When the second-generation head of one chemical and wood products concern sought financing for his first acquisition, he was afraid of disrupting the family business's traditional banking relationship. Yet he was stunned by the loan agreement offered by the company's longtime banker. "I couldn't understand most of it. And what I could understand, I didn't like," he recalls.

When he took the agreement to his board, "they were appalled," he says. Directors gave him the courage to apply at a competing bank, where he received much more favorable terms. To his surprise, he says, "Our old bank has been treating us even nicer now."

7. Challenging, Provocative Questions. At an effective board meeting, 80 percent of the sentences end in question marks. Many family businesses find challenging, provocative questions help them learn more, and learn it more quickly, than almost any other device. And the independent director, free from office politics, self-interest, and other sources of bias, can unearth good questions that may never even occur to management or family insiders. This process is not always comfortable, and it can mean extra management work, but it almost always improves the quality of decision making.

8. *Confidential and Empathic Counsel.* Family business owners have unusual empathy for each other. On an airplane or at a party, two family business owners usually manage to find each other and share stories. This almost instinctive relationship carries through to the boardroom, and it can be a unique resource to anyone facing issues too big, too sensitive, or too troubling to discuss with anyone else.

Family business owners often develop deep trust in their independent directors. One sought help from his board in deciding whether he should send his two young manager sons to an expensive, six-month executive education program. During a particularly difficult time for another family business leader, he unburdened himself at a board meeting, laying all his self-doubts on the table and gathering his directors' empathy and encouragement in return. A board's ability to help address those issues where business and emotion cross paths can prove invaluable.

A board can also help with personnel decisions that go to the very top of a family business. Often, the head of a family business may simply be incapable of providing effective leadership any longer; in other instances, the leader will be willing to move aside provided there is confidence that a suitable replacement will be named. In these and other like instances the objectivity and empathy of an independent board can be very helpful.

The empathy independent directors have for the leader and owners of a family business confronting an intense dilemma will enable them to lighten the mood in a way no others could.

9. *Creative Thinking and Decision Making.* The unique perspective of the boardroom can engender creative new approaches to old problems. Effective independent directors bring to the table the ability to see a problem from different points of view. The result is often a fresh and sometimes liberating perspective. To escape the demands of his business, Seth Brown, third-generation president of a family-held metal fasteners concern, likes to jump in his boat and sail far out into Lake Michigan. Distant from shore, and intent on the winds, he often thinks of fresh new solutions to problems back at the office. The same reasoning, Brown says, applies to the presence of independent directors on his board. "In closely held businesses, you really need that perspective," he says. "You've got to step away as often as you can, to ask yourself, 'What are we doing? What's going on here?' and reflect on that."

While the CEO might not hope for constant brilliance from the board, this forum offers the freedom to brainstorm ideas that evoke different perspectives, thinking laterally, drawing relationships among seemingly unrelated factors, and making connections among analogous situations or problems. All these are important parts of the creative process that will lead to better solutions.

Reasoning by analogy is an important technique to which an independent board is well suited. A well-chosen board will probably include people from businesses in some way analogous to the family's—in markets, distribution channels, industry structure, family stage, and so on. The board of a funeral home chain, for instance, might include the head of another business that syndicates new retail outlets, such as a restaurant chain, or home health care products and services.

As each director listens to the problem and the questions facing the company, they are filtered through personal experience. The result can be invaluable input into the decision-making process.

In essence, the board can help family businesses approach varied issues with fresh perspective and thinking—in effect, helping them to work *on*, not merely *in*, their business.

10. Valuable Corporate Relations. Many family businesses intent on improving planning and decision making at their companies discover their independent boards have an unforeseen benefit: better corporate relations with constituents ranging from employees, suppliers and customers to lenders and the community at large.

The senior management's willingness to be accountable to a board of respected peers carries great weight with employees, customers, and others. It is an emblem of senior management's dedication to the business and awareness of personal limitations—a commitment to professionalism. All these factors can help in recruiting top job candidates and retaining valued employees.

Perhaps most important, the existence of a respected board conveys the message to anyone with a stake in the company's future that the owners are interested in continuity and stability. It also lends major decisions credibility with employees and shareholders and other stakeholders. When directors have endorsed a new policy or a tough initiative, everyone knows it is not just a random thought by the proprietors.

A Social Argument

An active independent board can send a clear signal to all of a company's constituencies that the family shares certain fundamental core values of *review, accountability,* and *disclosure.* The mere existence of the board suggests the family is open-minded, unafraid to expose its vulnerabilities, and committed to the long-term success and perpetuation of the business rather than in short-term profit or perks to benefit the owners.

In a larger sense, the existence of an independent board is a symbol of the family's awareness that ownership is both a privilege and a responsibility. It signals consciousness of the responsibility of stewardship—not only to themselves, but to the community.

That is not just doing the right thing for the right thing's sake—there are pragmatic advantages as well. Banks and other suppliers can look more favorably on a family business that is committed to doing right by itself, its employees, and the community as a whole. This can carry powerful sway when financing and other like issues need to be addressed.

The Role of the Board in the Family Business

We believe the board of directors can play an invaluable role in the success of a family business. Just as management often has greater latitude in a family enterprise—for example, to take a temporary hit in profitability in order to invest for the long term—family company directors can play a uniquely helpful role. The family business board can go beyond typical boardroom conventions to explore broad questions of policy, philosophy, and planning, such as:

- Examining and helping to express the company's mission and philosophy.
- Assessing the organization's culture and determining its impact on the company's effort to achieve objectives.
- Ensuring the family and business have comprehensive plans for the future, from establishing a family vision to estate, succession, and strategic planning.
- Improving the quality of strategy. This implies more than strategic planning and evaluating strategic choices. It encompasses all that has to do with strategic thinking—assuring the long-term survival, development, and prosperity of the firm.

Many owners of small and medium-sized businesses set the mission, goals, and strategy for their businesses with limited input from outside the management team. Yet, setting the road map for an enterprise is a challenging task that can be better accomplished with external input. In our survey, the directors' most important role is helping management clarify and think through their strategic direction, and next in importance is serving as a sounding board for senior management in all areas of business. In another nationwide survey of private business owners by the National Association of Corporate Directors, most ranked "helping the CEO be effective"—including offering expertise, insisting on planning, and acting as confidant to the CEO—as the main reason to have an active board.

Value of Board to Family Business Leadership

- Give input on strategic direction.
- Serve as a sounding board for strategic management.
- Ensure owners' goals and objectives are clarified and considered.
- Ensure follow-through on plans and budgets.
- Provide objectivity on family business issues.
- Provide guidance and support on succession issues.

This does not mean directors are free to tinker with operations. Running the company is management's role. One experienced director enforces appropriate roles by interrupting the CEO when he gets into the operating details with his board: "Excuse me, but that's an operating matter. It doesn't belong before the board."

Nor should the board try to replace technical or management consultants or in-house experts. One rule of thumb suggests directors should never become involved in operations to the point that they feel they have made a decision.

Nevertheless, many owners believe the relative freedom of the private company environment enhances their board relationships. "With a public company board, directors have fiduciary responsibilities to so many stockholders, and so on, that they have to be very careful about what they say and do," says one owner, who also serves on several boards. In contrast, he says, "Our directors can express their true feelings and opinions about what we ought to do."

The Legal Role of the Board

Family business boards must also fulfill the legal duties of corporate directors. These legal mandates lay a firm foundation for the special opportunities discussed in greater detail later in this chapter. Most of the board's duties are set forth in general terms by the Model Business Corporations Act (MBCA). This legislation has been adopted in at least 35 states and reflects principles that also exist in most other states' laws.

According to the MBCA, "All corporate powers shall be exercised by or under the authority of, and the business and affairs of the corporation managed by or under the direction of, its board of directors, subject to any limitation set forth in the articles of incorporation." Beyond this blanket statement, the MBCA assigns the board responsibility to adopt or change corporate bylaws, approve amendments to the articles of incorporation, approve mergers, acquisitions and changes in capital structure, declare dividends, and elect corporate officers.

While fulfilling these legal responsibilities is a fundamental duty of directors, the well-chosen board is far too valuable to be used only for custodial and fiduciary purposes.

In the private company setting, owners have the latitude to decide how they are going to use the board, and can structure the board with the appropriate individuals and agenda to provide support in desired areas. Some of the areas where boards can be most effective in supporting the business are listed below.

How a Board Can Support a Business

- Serve as a sounding board to the CEO
- Establish objectives and policies
- Help management make decisions
- Share experiences from other industry/company environments
- Protect shareholders
- Help in times of crisis to ensure company survival
- Select the CEO
- Lend credibility and enhance company image
- Promote the company
- Act as arbitrator
- Report to shareholders

While this list is comprehensive, it does not demonstrate or detail the complete range of ways in which a board may fulfill a variety of important functions and responsibilities. In the remainder of the chapter, we will take a look at the roles a board can play in helping the family business achieve its potential.

Reflecting on the Fundamentals

Plato said: "The life which is unexamined is not worth living." Bearing that lofty thought in mind, few things can refresh management's and owners' perspectives on the distinctive strengths of the company and its culture more than the involvement of an experienced board. By observing and pointing out some of these special attributes, directors often act as catalysts to the important process of weighing and articulating the company's mission, philosophy, and organizational culture.

Balancing Stakeholder Interests

CEOs often make Solomon-like decisions—complex choices about how to allocate the company's resources among the multitude of constituents it serves. Sometimes, they may struggle with an important decision due to the different ramifications a given choice may have on the business and the family; at other times, CEOs may not have considered the ramifications for stakeholders, such as suppliers, or industry regulators.

A wise director can help a CEO weigh the importance to the company of all stakeholders—not only the shareholders, but also the company's employees, customers, suppliers, and the community. Each plays an important role in the company's fortunes. And the interests of each need to be measured against those of the shareholders and the company itself—a difficult balancing act.

If the customer is not satisfied, the growth of the business will slow, and employees, suppliers, and shareholders will suffer. If employees are not satisfied and productive, then resulting personnel and product-quality problems can be detrimental to product or service in the short term, and to corporate performance over time. And if family owners are not content, they may become reluctant to support the bold reinvestments needed to sustain and grow operations.

To some degree, one can even argue that each constituent (someone that has a demand or expectation of the company—a customer, shareholder, employee, supplier, community member) is in competition with all others. Lowering a price for customers may reduce net returns to shareholders. If suppliers are squeezed to make up the difference, how will that affect those crucial long-term relationships? Or, if increasing pay to ensure a high-caliber workforce requires an increase in prices, will customers defect to a competitor's product? Such stakeholder issues sometimes surface in ways a CEO may never anticipate. The board can help the CEO become aware of stakeholder conflicts, examine trade-offs they are making, and debate whether they are the right ones.

A difficult trade-off arose for the CEO of one family business when he realized he needed to raise salaries to retain top management and attract new managers. With the help of his board, he weighed the problem and decided to hold down dividends for a few years to free up cash. The board helped him and the rest of the ownership group to see a reduction in near-term income as a reasonable trade-off for the sake of an improved management team.

Balancing divergent stakeholder interests is a difficult challenge. No CEO can keep all corporate stakeholders happy all the time. But with the help of an active, effective board, the chances of maintaining a healthy balance improve significantly.

The Corporate Mission Statement

The corporate mission statement defines the company's business and expresses company goals, competitive strengths, and strategy. It may specify target customers and markets; identify principal products, services, or core technologies; express commitments; articulate sources of corporate identity; or describe the firm's desired public image.

Mission statements can take a variety of forms. They might express such goals as becoming a household word, achieving a target-market share, serving a specific market, or capitalizing on competitive advantages.

An effective board can serve several purposes in developing and/or improving the corporate mission statement. First, directors often highlight the need for a mission statement by raising fundamental questions. "What are you in business to accomplish?" directors may ask. "What businesses, markets, and goals are important to you?" In situations where a mission has not been clearly defined, the board can offer examples and counsel that can help the management team tackle this unfamiliar and intimidating task. Directors can suggest a variety of methods: The CEO might organize a management retreat specifically for that purpose, or hire a consultant to facilitate the process. While the board does not have responsibility for defining the mission, it should take responsibility for ensuring that a clearly defined and compelling mission is in place.

Directors can also help with the substance of the document, pushing management to crystallize thoughts and ideas, focusing management energy on this important task and firming up plans for execution. In addition, the board should periodically review the mission statement, as this should be a "living document" that serves to continually sharpen the focus of the business.

Finally, the board should ensure the mission statement is used as a tool to guide major corporate decisions. Any major corporate move—an acquisition, the startup of a new product line, personnel reorganization—should be evaluated to ensure consistency with the defined mission.

The Corporate Values Statement

In many cases, the mission statement will incorporate a section on corporate values, which are the beliefs and principles that guide the company. In a family-owned business, the values statement, whether standing alone or part of the mission, can be a relatively personal document that reflects the character and style of its owners. As a company grows and evolves, the values statement can ensure continuity with the legacy of the founders and create a greater sense of identity and resolve.

One company's values statement might stress its pride in retaining employees and attracting their friends and children. Another might emphasize the commitment of shareholders to perpetuating the company as a private business. Yet another might underscore the importance of the owners' partnership with suppliers, customers, and community.

With their unique insights, directors can often encourage business owners to make the values statement a distinctive and meaningful document. Directors can also offer constructive and confidential reactions to drafts of the document. Additionally, directors can encourage the ownership group to develop separate and distinct family mission and values statements that identify core values, objectives, and other goals that are particularly important to owners. The statement of the owners' purpose and goals allows directors to fully understand owners' desires for the business. When both mission and values statements are present, directors can be responsible for supporting alignment between ownership and business goals.

Assessing the Organizational Culture

Corporate culture has taken on new meaning as managers gain greater understanding of its relevance to corporate performance. In fact, corporate culture—the shared values and expectations of the organization—can profoundly affect the company's ability to accomplish goals, implement strategies, and fulfill objectives.

McKee Foods Corp. is an iconic family business success story. The manufacturer of Little Debbie's snacks, the business has grown into a 6,000-employee concern with more than $1 billion in annual international sales. While the company achieved this level of success without the input of independent directors, the family owners believed that adding independent directors to the board would be crucial factor in their ongoing success. Company president Mike McKee says those independent board members—added in 2008—provide the company with objective insight while instilling a greater sense of accountability.

"We wanted the advice of accomplished professionals," McKee says. "Before we had a board of directors with outsiders, we really didn't feel we had to answer to anybody. There's a higher sense of accountability with a board."

The presence of a board that includes independent directors also touched on one issue of organizational culture. As Seventh Day Adventists, the McKees observe the Sabbath on Saturdays, shuttering operations on a day when most other companies continue to hum.

The board's reaction: If it's important to you, it's important. As McKee notes, the directors were quick to recognize the importance of honoring the family's values in its business operations, even if it meant a potential disadvantage versus their competition.

"We made it very clear in the selection process that our values were important," says McKee. "We did a really good job of selecting the people who sit on our board. They ask good questions and can validate those things that you might only feel in the pit of your stomach."

An effective board can also observe, and articulate opinions on, special aspects of the corporate culture that may have gone unnoticed by the business's owners. Directors can offer suggestions on emphasizing and preserving aspects of the culture that hold potential business or personal value. The board can also spot areas of cultural dysfunction or contradictions in the culture.

One CEO, for instance, was guiding his company through the transition from entrepreneurial to professional management. Like most entrepreneurs, he had long run the company by the force of his personality. For years, his relatively closed, paternalistic management style had been part of the company's culture.

As the company grew, the board began to see the value of adding first-class professional managers. But even as the CEO began recruiting a few top people for key positions, he unconsciously resisted a crucial related step: creating a sense of greater openness, sharing of information, and participation in corporate culture—all necessary elements that contribute to genuinely professional management.

The idea of sharing financial information was anathema to him. Like many business owners, he had always thought it an unwarranted violation of his privacy. With the help of directors, he was able to see this cultural contradiction, discuss it confidentially, and gradually overcome it.

Of course, the culture of the family business is often a very personal matter. In some cases, that culture is intense and unique, reflecting the owners' personalities, family history, and heritage. These qualities pose special opportunities for creating a sense of identity and importance among employees and other constituencies.

The unique intensity that can characterize family company culture can also make transitions during major corporate changes particularly difficult, such as management succession. An effective board can help ease such changes, pointing out areas of inflexibility, and supporting new managers through the transition.

Assessing the organizational culture yields continual benefits once the CEO and family owners are especially aware of that culture. A trusted board can help management examine corporate culture, identifying the benefits it brings to the company and determining if there are negative implications of the culture that may need to be addressed. The board can also help the CEO understand the impact his or her personal style may have on the culture and the potential unintended consequences. While it is exceedingly difficult for a management team to provide feedback on personal style to their boss, the board can often provide insights to the CEO in a collegial and matter-of-fact way.

To sum up, company boards at family-controlled enterprises, free from some of the pressures and obligations that burden public company directors, are able to fulfill special opportunities to help improve business performance and decision making.

Directors can encourage, and help produce, a statement of the company's mission and philosophy of management. They can help assess and strengthen the organization's culture and its impact on performance. The board can prove valuable in meeting specific challenges and handling singular opportunities—tasks that will be addressed in the chapter 4.

4

The Special Value of Independent Directors to the Family Business

To this point, we have focused on the value of the board as a whole in ensuring the family business is well run. Generally speaking, an active board that is appropriately focused on strategic issues is an asset to the family business, regardless of the composition of the board.

Yet, due to the special challenges of family business ownership, we strongly believe in the value of independent directors to the family business board. These individuals can add value in a number of ways, from providing objectivity on delicate subjects such as compensation and succession planning, to injecting an outside perspective, to serving as mentors for next generation of management. This opinion is borne out by our research: Only 54 percent of respondents with family boards felt their boards were effective or highly effective, compared to 83 percent with two or more independent directors, and 96 percent who had a majority of independent directors.

Board Insight

A board of directors with independent representation has an important role to play in providing objectivity and oversight to ensure that difficult topics are addressed in a manner that protects the long-term viability of the business as well as the family relationships that may be directly or indirectly impacted.

Murray Berstein has overseen the growth of Nixon Uniform Service and Medical Wear since the reorganization of corporate assets that resulted when he split the business with his former partner in the late 1990s. Since then, the New Castle, Delaware, company has averaged annual growth in excess of 15 percent. As the sole voting stockholder, Berstein felt that having an independent board could provide invaluable support to his three sons in the short term, should something happen to him, and over time as he transitioned the business to them. "For one thing, if something happened to me, I wanted to have outsiders in place with an objective interest in the business," he says. "But they also had me focus on future needs, such as ways to establish succession planning for my three sons. For instance, to help them get a handle on what they would recommend, they had my sons sit in on board meetings. That way, they would get to know them."

Berstein's advice to those pursuing independent directors—set high standards and seek out the very best people you can find. "Our independent directors brought a lot of professionalism to the company. They helped us identify niches that were simply not profitable. With the right directors, you're receiving valuable input from day one."

Family business leaders face a special set of privileges and challenges: balancing the interests of the family against those of the business; grappling with the divergent roles of family members, managers, and shareholders; planning for the future of both the business and the family; and possibly making a transition to nonfamily leadership or ownership. Any of these challenges, if mishandled, can sink a family business.

"One of the most important things that the introduction of independent directors does is that it immediately changes the entire dynamic of the discussion," says our colleague, Craig Aronoff, cofounder of the Family Business Consulting Group. "The discussions of family issues and business issues are immediately separated into their proper venues. Moreover, the board comes to recognize what are genuine business issues and what are family issues. Then the board can put the family and business back together again."

A board with strong independent representation can help smooth the way to constructive decision making. The objective, confidential, and caring counsel of an effective board can help the family business leaders and owners effectively address such issues as succession planning, mentoring younger family members, and other essential responsibilities. A board is also crucial in spurring the adoption and integration of the many other long-range plans needed in the family business: the estate plan, the strategic plan, and the family continuity plan (all of which will be discussed later in this chapter).

Research on family businesses concludes that an active independent board is one of the most critical elements in their success and, in certain cases, their very survival. Let's take a look at some of those special benefits.

Planning for Orderly Management Succession

For some business leaders, relinquishing the reins of the family business is one of the hardest challenges they will confront in life. The prospect can raise thorny issues that no manager relishes, from choosing among one's children to planning a diminished role for oneself. The overlap of business and family priorities is challenging to navigate and can become even more complex at succession points beyond the first and second generations, with more related parties in the mix.

It is, therefore, not a surprise to learn that many family business leaders delay or avoid succession planning, often with devastating consequences. Laird Norton Tyee's "Family to Family" survey reports that less than 30 percent of respondents had succession plans in place, even though nearly 60 percent of the majority shareholders in the survey were age 55 or older; nearly 30 percent were 65 or older. Further, less than 40 percent of these businesses had a successor preparing for the transition.

An independent board can be invaluable to the succession process in several ways: ensuring that a succession plan is in place well in advance of the time it might be needed; helping the current leader examine various options; ensuring the successor is being adequately prepared, and helping plan for, and completing, the process. No other resource provides as comprehensive a source of support to help the company and family achieve continuity as a business passes from generation to generation.

The Board as a Safety Net

A crucial role for the family business board is as a type of insurance policy for the business in the event of a succession crisis, such as the death or disability of the CEO or a key owner. Such crises often breed hasty and, sometimes, disastrous reactions, such as an untimely sale of the business or the ascent of a person ill-qualified to lead.

An effective board is equipped with knowledge of the family's goals, values and philosophy, coupled with an absence of any vested interest in selling the business or grabbing power. Thus, independent directors are uniquely able to play a guardian or facilitator's role, evaluating the alternatives and counseling family members on the best course of action going forward.

Aid in Timely Succession Planning

A board can be instrumental in raising the succession issue at the proper time. Typically, that is several years before the CEO's or chair's planned retirement, and often before he or she even recognizes the need. Some families ask their directors to help them identify the appropriate time for them to step down.

For others, the issue is much more difficult to face. This is how one such entrepreneur's oldest son, who is now president of the 125-employee family business, describes the role of an independent board in his succession: "I wouldn't be in this office right now if it weren't for the board. Dad had to overcome some gigantic barriers to decide to finally name a successor to the presidency, to let go and step back.

"It was obvious to me that we needed an objective perspective, a getting beyond the old tapes—how I behaved when I was 13 years old affecting how he sees my performance now, that sort of thing. The board helped define the issues in getting to the point where Dad could make a decision. I think the board was constantly pushing my dad too: 'So there are a couple of things you don't like about him. But who else is going to take over? So what if he does this or that? It's not going to undo the company.'"

Today, this successful family business is running well, and the independent board is continuing to smooth the succession process, defusing tensions between father and son and helping each prepare for the future.

Helping Family Business Leaders Examine Their Options

For some retiring business leaders, weighing leadership alternatives raises significant and confusing questions. What strengths are needed in my successor, based on the business's future strategic challenges? Are family members capable of taking over? If so, how can we select among them? How can we ensure they are getting the challenging professional opportunities that will help them prepare for future business leadership? If family members are not an option, should we look to nonfamily leadership or consider selling?

In the privacy of the boardroom, the business leaders can examine such questions honestly and confidentially, without fear of alarming or hurting other family members or employees. The board can also help to analyze the business's future leadership needs and weigh candidates' qualifications in light of those conclusions.

Often, independent directors can provide the necessary missing link—a vote of confidence, a new idea, affirmation of the CEO's judgments or instincts—that the CEO or ownership group needs to proceed. Other times, the board can reassure the business owner or owners by suggesting alternatives that might have been too difficult to promote alone.

Help Planning the Succession Process

A smooth management transition does not happen overnight. "Succession is not an event. It's a process," says one company chair. "Ours started ten years ago and will take three more years." This process requires careful planning and preparation.

Many CEOs and owning families wonder what method is best when choosing a successor. Groom the leading candidate? Hire a consultant to guide the selection process? Let a few top candidates "self-select" by competing within the business? Split up the business? We find that half of family business management successions involve more than one offspring, increasing the complexity of the task.

Board Insight

Directors can be of great help in defining the process for choosing a successor; in moderating this process to keep it healthy, deliberate, and open; and in providing support to both the chair and the candidates. Here, the concept of "fair process" comes into play—a careful, well-thought-out procedure that ensures the selection process is as transparent and objective as it possibly can be. Without the presence and input of independent directors, a family business may find it difficult to carry out fair process when trying to choose a suitable successor.

"I saw an outside board as an opportunity to get help with the selection of the next CEO," says the owner of a locksmith-supply distribution concern with three children working in the business. "It's very difficult to separate your roles as father and boss. I didn't really feel capable of making a decision purely on a business basis. I felt my wife, although her judgment is very good, would get involved emotionally. And if I went to my children and asked, 'Who should run this company?' I'd have no volunteers. None of them really wants to say yet, 'Dad, I'll take your place.' Again, it's my being the father that gets in the way."

In the case of larger family businesses, a more formal structure should be put in place to manage the succession process. Some businesses will use an owners' council to oversee issues related to ownership, such as setting dividend policies or overseeing family member employment and ascension through the ranks. Others may create a succession task force encompassing representatives of the ownership group, the human resources function, and a board member to oversee the leadership-succession process.

In any of these models, independent directors provide objectivity and also lend credibility and authority to the process by ratifying the owner or owners' choice. The half-owner of one family business says the board helped the family select a son-in-law over his and his brother's two sons as the heir apparent—a decision they knew was right but was still extremely difficult. "It was a bitter pill," he recalls, but the board's approval helped make it palatable for everyone concerned.

Help in Preparing the Successor

Once a potential successor or successors have been identified, independent directors can be invaluable in helping prepare the individual or individuals for senior management.

The board can keep an objective eye on the learning opportunities afforded a successor. Often, directors discover that successors are not being challenged enough—that they need to be thrown in over their heads to develop skills and discover the depths of their capabilities. The board can help suggest new challenges and leadership-development opportunities.

Interaction with the board can help the successors develop a new level of professionalism and a sense of accountability. For instance, they can be asked to give reports to the board and consider directors' feedback. However, it is worth noting that when the succession event is several years away, it is usually best not to make the successor a board member, as there still may be issues the CEO needs to discuss without the successor present.

But as the CEO approaches retirement, the board can provide a formal vehicle for the succession process. First, the successor can be integrated gradually into board meetings, eventually as a member and finally as CEO. In some cases, the CEO will move immediately or in a few years into the position of chair. At this point, of course, the successor begins managing the board and preparing the agenda.

This process provides many opportunities for grooming and encouraging the successor. A director of one large industrial services concern recalls that when the founder's daughter first joined the board as heir apparent, she was timid and overwhelmed at the impending responsibility. However, the directors saw that she was also extremely capable, and they encouraged her and mentored her to ask questions and develop self-confidence. Today, her self-esteem has blossomed to the point where she is eager to take the reins at the appropriate time.

Some family business leaders ask independent directors to serve as mentors. The successor may visit a director's business, learning about management systems, human resources, training, and other aspects of professional management. Often, successors are more receptive to learning from the experiences of directors outside the family and in this way achieve the added benefit of seeing how a different business is managed.

Other directors meet informally with successors on the job, offering advice and guidance. One director of a family-held food concern periodically stops at the company on his way home from work to talk to the owner's sons "about a particular problem they may have, in sales or marketing or operations," says the CEO. "When my oldest son wanted to start retail units within department stores, we had no idea how a department store works. But this director did. He was able to give him pro forma financials and help him organize the unit."

The board can also be an excellent vehicle to provide peers who are close to the successor's age that can serve as role models. Many family business successors lack helpful peers because they tend to assume positions of influence and responsibility far earlier than their peers from school or the community. They also tend to be better off financially. Younger successful business leaders who serve on the family's board can serve as a role model to successors from the successor's generation. By selecting one or two directors who are closer in age to the successor and who may be entrepreneurs or family business successors themselves, the board can provide highly influential role models for achievement, initiative, and responsibility.

Directors also can provide access to a network of business leaders and other successors to support the successors' leadership development. In meeting and getting to know these people, many of whom may have gone through a succession process in a family business themselves, the successor can learn about the many important dimensions of family business leadership that are not taught in textbooks—not only good management skills but leadership in the family and community and social, civic, and philanthropic obligations.

Finally, directors can help decide when a successor is ready to take over. "Quite honestly, I'm anxious to get out of my spot," says the head of one family-held distribution company. "I'd like to let someone else be CEO. But when I discussed this with the board about a year and a half ago, they didn't feel my oldest son was ready then. We will take it up again in another year or so."

Monitoring the Final Stages

The final stages of succession can be the most difficult. Many CEOs have a hard time really letting go. Yet, it is almost impossible for a successor to say, "You're getting too involved. You're second-guessing me too much," or "You should be working through me, Dad, instead of going around me all the time."

One helpful succession strategy is a gradual transfer of responsibility, with the successor slowly taking on more duties and obligations. An independent board can prove very useful in this process, not merely by setting up the overall schedule but also by monitoring progress and performance to make certain the successor is coming up to speed and the incumbent leader is genuinely relinquishing responsibilities.

Directors can greatly increase the effectiveness of the new CEO during this period. Sometimes, the board can provide a suitable place for family members to let off steam in what is often a tense environment. Other times, it can provide a much-needed sense of professionalism and credibility to the new generation of management. "Without these directors" says the third-generation head of an industrial products concern, "I would still be the son reporting back to the parents."

Directors can also keep family tensions from blocking important management decisions. One second-generation CEO, who just took over the family business from his father, says, "I'm convinced that my dad will never say to me, 'You've arrived!' That's just the way he is. He's never quite satisfied. But the board has helped me in a lot of ways. We have an old plant in Cleveland that we've outgrown. If I walked into Dad's office and said, 'Dad, we've got to do something about Cleveland,' the first thing he'd ask me is, 'How much is it going to cost? We can't look at that kind of spending.'

"But when I introduced that issue at a board meeting, we could bring it out in the open and discuss it logically. My dad asked the board, 'Do you realize how much this is going to cost?' And one of the directors said, 'But, Jack, this is your business you're talking about. You can't look only at cost. You've got to grow your business.' The board agreed that it made sense, so we're going ahead in Cleveland."

Sometimes, independent directors can help the founder step back. During an informal annual weekend retreat, one

CEO says his independent directors helped him make the decision to step aside to the chair from the presidency of his business, clearing the way for younger successors. Board members helped him see the need, he says, and to recognize his own desire to pursue other interests as well. Board members can even be instrumental in helping outgoing CEOs to envision a future to which they can happily retire. They can help identify and create an ongoing meaningful role within the business as board chair or ambassador to customers or employees, while ensuring the role does not create conflict with the new leadership or confusion with employees or other stakeholders.

In cases where the outgoing CEO takes over the chair role, the independent directors can help to ensure the chair focuses on managing the business of the board, as opposed to managing the CEO or business operations. The transition from CEO to chair can be a difficult culture change for some leaders, and one that benefits from objective oversight.

Help with Organizational Succession

One aspect of succession that is often neglected is organizational succession—the changes that new leadership will bring throughout the company. As a family business contemplates management succession, broader questions arise: How will the new CEO change the nature of the organization? What does this change mean for the development and promotion of other family members in the company and for key non-family managers? How can we provide for a continuing evolution of leadership? How do we reassure employees that the strengths of our culture will be preserved?

Some family-owned businesses and their boards of directors establish a succession task force to help address the issue of organizational adaptation. This group can prove exceedingly effective in making certain that all persons affected by organizational succession receive complete and appropriate training to prepare them for their new roles and ensure they are being adequately developed for any future role to which they may aspire. This committee is often involved in tracking the progress of next-generation family members as succession candidates, ensuring they gain the experience required to be well-rounded leaders.

Help with Ongoing Business Issues

Financial Matters

Even the closest-knit family can fray under the financial pressures raised by business ownership. Compensation of family members working in the business, dividend policy, valuation of the firm, benefits and perks for family members—all are issues that can fragment a family.

Consider the case of this family, for whom shared decision making was nothing new. Even when the ten children were very small, the family held weekly meetings on issues of common concern. "We would sit around the kitchen table, with the littlest one still sucking his thumb," recalls one who is now the CEO of the family's highly successful business.

"My mother would read the minutes of the last kitchen table meeting, and we'd approve them. Then, there would be suggestions—things like, 'I don't want to wash the dishes anymore,' or, 'I think we should only have to wash them once a week.' We have always been pretty close and able to overcome our differences."

But as the siblings grew up and assumed joint ownership of the fast-growing company their father had founded, unprecedented tensions arose. Although management bonuses had long been based on a percentage of profit, some brothers and sisters not working in the company began to resent what they viewed as windfall compensation that their three siblings in management were receiving.

"We had brothers and sisters running to the internet to research the typical pay for somebody in this industry," the

CEO says. Another brother who decided to seek his fortune elsewhere wanted to sell all his stock, placing heavy financial demands on the company. "Emotions were starting to run high, and feelings were getting hurt at some of our family meetings," the CEO recalls.

For this family, injecting independent directors into the decision making process was the answer. The board helped restructure management compensation, cutting salaries and capping bonuses, but adding long-term stock options and certain perquisites for managers. Directors also helped lay out a stock buyback plan. Family members were grateful for help with these issues, the CEO says: "The board has freed us from the burden" of battling through the issues within the family.

In some cases, directors can offer information about what certain kinds of jobs are worth, what perks and incentives are typical, and other significant details. In other cases, the board will recommend and help review the findings of a reputable compensation consultant.

Ultimately, directors can bring objectivity to potentially explosive issues. Independent directors are particularly valuable in cases where owners' interests clearly diverge. One business owner recalls acquiring a family-held company that had been doing well under the leadership of the second-generation owner-manager, who was reinvesting all business proceeds back into the company. But the CEO's mother and sister—the other two owners of this company—were dissatisfied with their returns from the business, so they sold out. "They got tired of getting nothing out of the business," the owner recalls. "If I were a passive holder, I would feel more comfortable having an independent board. Directors can be responsive to a mix of outsiders and insiders and ensure adequate returns."

Successor and Next-generation Evaluation

Evaluating the performance of family members in the business can raise all kinds of conflicts for a family business.

Nonfamily executives may be reluctant to provide thorough performance feedback to prospective successors, as these individuals could one day be their bosses. As a result, family members may suffer from a lack of thorough, objective feedback on their performance.

Board Insight

Frequently, family-owned businesses create a Human Resources Committee to guide career development and provide feedback to family employees. One or two independent directors will typically serve on that committee, along with one or two human resource professionals.

Business leaders may struggle endlessly with important personnel decisions because of a lack of complete information on relevant candidates.

Independent directors can provide valuable input and support to a CEO in this process and also lend credibility to any necessary evaluations. Many CEOs even ask their boards to evaluate their own performance each year, measuring them against the goals and objectives they have identified for themselves.

Balancing competing roles

On occasion, family business CEOs might feel they are playing the entire cast of a Broadway play—alone. The roles range from parent to shareholder, from president and chief manager to community leader, from employer to entrepreneur.

Nowhere as effectively as inside the boardroom can business leaders be reminded that they wear multiple hats. Independent directors are uniquely able to help the leader manage this complex balancing act and to point out conflicts. The board may say, "You're sounding like a father on this question, and it's a management issue," or, "It's great to plow every cent back into the business, Hank, but you need to start thinking about your own retirement, too."

For instance, one CEO found it easy to neglect returns to the business' shareholders (himself and his wife). But his paternal instincts led him to pay enormous salaries and bonuses to family members and others in the business year after year. While his employees were overjoyed and he felt gratified, he was threatening the long-term viability of the business, not to mention risking his own future financial security.

Another business leader plowed so much capital into a son's new business unit that he undercut the company's other operations. He was "so enamored of this project that his child had embarked on, that he was risking the goose that laid the golden egg," says an independent director, who raised questions about the allocation of resources.

Often, all a CEO needs is to be reminded of his divergent responsibilities and made aware when interests clash. Truly independent directors provide an invaluable service when they simply point out the conflict of perspectives involved in a given decision confronting the family business owner.

A Stabilizing Influence for the Family

An independent board can also have a stabilizing influence on the family business, playing a role one family business CEO likens to "a balance wheel" in times of high emotion or conflict. Family members often feel foolish airing petty squabbles before esteemed directors. "We have these respected and accomplished people on our board, and we're sitting here arguing about the company car?" a family member might wonder.

Putting a contested issue on the board's agenda can defuse arguments. After one family business board had discussed such a matter, one of the owners present said, "You don't realize how many problems you solved for us by merely letting us hear you all talk about it!" While the directors had not been aware that the family members were deeply divided, their debate lent new perspective that was helpful to family members.

One business owner grappling with estate planning found his board an invaluable resource: "The board could certainly be a wonderful arbitrator if the family were in a life-and-death battle. But I find the mere existence of the board keeps things from coming to that—to the right-or-wrong, win-lose, Charlie-versus-Julie" kind of showdown.

Directors can serve the same lightning-rod function for family members who need to air their goals, ambitions, frustrations, or concerns privately, without consulting each other or their parents. The board can also break deadlocks between family members.

One family business leader in an uneasy partnership with his brother says independent directors enabled the contentious siblings to work together in relative peace for years. Whenever a conflict arose, the brothers laid position papers before the board and agreed to abide by its decision. Without the help of directors, "We might have shot each other," the CEO quips.

Board Insight

While the board might mediate a family dispute occasionally, this practice should be avoided and should rarely be the role of one director alone.

Ideally, a director's role stops short of forging alliances or working as mediator-in-chief. The director can discreetly urge resolution of the conflict, for instance, or indicate sticking points that might be missed by the combatants. Certainly, taking sides in such a battle typically marks the end of the director's effectiveness. "That would be like trying to dive into a marriage," says one CEO.

Family Education

Independent directors can play a valuable role in educating next-generation leadership. In fact, educational roles reach beyond business leadership demonstrating effective shared decision making —a skill crucial to healthy family interaction. Learning how a mutually respectful group tries to build consensus can also be critical to the future functioning of the business if a large number of family members become involved in management.

The board can be a conduit of information from the business to the family. Reading board agendas, observing meetings, and attending social gatherings with directors all provide unique opportunities for the family to learn about the business. The boardroom can be a tremendous educational environment for family members unschooled in strategic and organizational issues.

The Board as a Symbol of Continuity and Dedication

The common stereotypes about privately held companies— that they are highly secretive and have a propensity for conflicts of interest—are applied with even more critical force to the family business. Judging by examples highlighted in the media and popular literature, one would assume that most family businesses are torn apart by sibling battles or plundered and abandoned by negligent, self-obsessed owners. Anyone who remembers the old television program "Dallas" knows all too well the infighting that occurs when blood relatives try to run an insular family operation.

But "Dallas" was fiction—and so is the perception of the family business as a ruthless, no-holds-barred war to the death. The existence of a board with respected independent directors can go a long way to countering such misconceptions, reassuring all concerned that the family is attending to the long-term best interests of the business. The board sends a message to suppliers, customers, and the community that the family intends to make succession an orderly event rather than a dramatic accident or knee-jerk postscript. It also conveys a signal that the owners are accountable, open, vulnerable, and aware of their own fallibility.

For many business leaders, these are values well worth conveying to the next generation. "Hopefully, this idea of accountability is ingrained in my kids now," says one CEO with an active independent board. "They have seen me do it for five years now."

The active, independent board holds special benefits for the family business. It can help with all aspects of management succession: planning the process, making the selection, preparing the successor, and monitoring the final stages of the transition. Directors can also act as a valuable insurance policy for a spouse, offering objective and well-informed counsel in the event of the business owner's sudden death or disability.

The independent board can offer objective advice on such potentially sensitive issues as family compensation, dividend policy, and benefits. It can help business owners manage and distinguish among their many roles. Often, the mere existence of the board also serves as a catalyst for important planning efforts, including the strategic, succession, estate, and family continuity plans.

Finally, an effective board can be an invaluable resource to the family, helping elevate the debate, educate family members, and resolve conflicts. It can provide a role model for skills and values, such as shared decision making and professional management that can greatly help the family's efforts to perpetuate the business.

5

The Vital Role of the Board in Family Business Continuity Planning

A leader with exceptional integrity and a clear vision for his company, Charles Collat, Sr., was instrumental in helping build Mayer Electric Supply into a $680 million concern in the southeastern United States. However, his longstanding presence made the issue of succession a delicate one to address—something the company's advisory board helped to solve.

"By the early 1990s, my father really needed to remove his shadow from the business—he really didn't realize the influence he had," says Nancy Goedecke, who now serves as the company's chair. "As a first step in implementing our succession plan, our board suggested that he physically remove himself from the company's premises."

Although Goedecke says her father's first reaction was one of "being put out to pasture," the fact that the recommendation came from a board comprised in part of independent directors helped convince Collat it was the right move to make—which, in time, became evident. He now serves as Mayer's chair emeritus. "He's actually been quite happy," says Goedecke. "He's still engaged and involved, but having him no longer in the building has allowed a nonfamily member to step up to the plate and take over the presidency."

Planning for the future of the family business involves a complex set of interrelated decisions. At its best, a family business is a tapestry of entrepreneurship, industry, and enterprise interwoven with the family's heritage, values, and dreams. Keeping those close-knit patterns in harmony requires a unique blend of long-range plans. Four distinct elements make up the foundation of family business planning:

1. The *strategic plan*, to ensure the business's future health
2. The *succession plan*, to assure orderly leadership change
3. The *estate* or *personal financial plan*, to provide for the owners' future security
4. The *family continuity plan*, an overarching statement of the family's philosophy and ownership vision that weaves together elements of all the other plans.

The presence of an independent board can serve as a catalyst to the planning process. An effective board will raise questions about all these aspects of the family business's future. Directors will be reluctant to address major business issues without knowing how they relate to the owners' overall vision and objectives. If the family has not yet thought through these issues, questions from the board will help clarify the importance of this planning for the long-term sustainability of the business and the family. Comments one family business CEO, "When we put the board in place, one of the first strategic questions put on the table was a potential acquisition. The independent directors turned to me and said 'How do the owners feel about acquisitions? What level of risk are they willing to take on? Would they be willing to forego a dividend to finance this acquisition?' At that point, I realized we had some work to do as an ownership group!" Once these plans are in place, the effective director will continually rely on the information and insights therein to weigh issues that come before the board.

The Strategic Plan

Planning a business's strategy and goals is the responsibility of management, not the board. However, directors can help get the process under way by raising the questions such a plan should answer. They also can bring invaluable experience and perspective to the process and help avoid certain pitfalls.

That has been the case at a publishing concern Rodale, Inc.: "In my first board meeting, I said, 'Here's what I think the major issues are,'" says CEO Maria Rodale. "One of the board members recommended a strategic planning consultant that we are going to use. We will involve the board in the planning process, but we don't want them to author the plan. The management team needs to own it because they are accountable for making it happen."

Board involvement in strategic planning can head off a number of potential pitfalls. For instance, if the plan is a product of the top management group, the CEO risks getting a plan based on what employees think the CEO wants to hear. Another risk in this approach is that the document can be so diluted by the process of making it acceptable to everyone that it lacks excitement or value for anyone. Board review is an excellent antidote for these problems.

Similarly, the directors can serve as an oversight mechanism to ensure that the strategic plan is aligned with ownership goals. If the business is not capable of delivering on owners' goals in the near term, the board can communicate its concerns to the owners about the viability of their expectations.

Because the role of the board in overseeing strategy is so crucial, we will focus on it in more detail later in this chapter.

The Succession Plan

The succession plan answers the highly sensitive and confidential questions, "Who is eligible to succeed me?" and "What should be my role once I have left my current position of leadership in the business?" These two issues must be decided in concert, and a board is uniquely able to address both without bias. Until a succession plan is developed, directors are likely to raise the issue frequently: How is the organization evolving? How are leaders developing? Put rather bluntly: What would happen if the CEO got hit by a truck?

The Estate Plan

All business owners need to provide for their financial futures as well as the futures of other family members. To be helpful in this regard directors need some knowledge of the owners' financial resources and future cash needs to anticipate capital demands on the business. Thus, a good board will raise questions about the owners' estate plans and often provide valuable help in reviewing options for retirement, transfer of stock or other assets, and long-term personal financial security.

For instance, one owner asked his directors, "What basic philosophies of personal asset management should I consider? How much income should I shelter from taxes? How much insurance do I need?"

It is also worth noting that many estates related to a family business are anything but straightforward: They can involve dozens of people and tiers of relatives of all ages. The more complicated an estate becomes, the more valuable is an independent board's role in helping ensure that all needs are fairly met and the business's best interests are protected.

The Family Continuity Plan

This fourth plan brings the other three plans together. As a statement of the family's mission, philosophy, ownership vision, and goals for the business, it maps out the family's role in the business, identifies the goals of individual family members, and formalizes and defines the family's commitment to the company's future. Drafting such a plan affords the family an opportunity to discuss family goals and business opportunities, and to formulate an overriding family philosophy—particularly with respect to how the family envisions ownership transfer in the future. Once complete, the family continuity plan can guide both the family and the board in helping shape the future of the company. With these four plans in place, a family business has done as complete a job as possible of planning for successful perpetuation of the business.

While directors often serve as catalysts to begin forming these distinct plans, they also can be helpful in weighing implicit tradeoffs. The process is certain to give rise to some competition for resources. For example, estate planning may require drawing funds from the business to ensure the owners' future financial security. Succession planning overlaps here as well, because family members not employed in the business may be treated differently in the estate plan. A board can help manage the needs of active and inactive owners as well as those of several generations. An independent board provides objective oversight to the process of balancing these competing priorities, leading to greater satisfaction in the outcome among all stakeholders.

Help with Strategic Planning: Pitfalls of Family Businesses

Strategy is essentially a structured way of thinking about the business. An effective board is uniquely able to contribute to the development and execution of strategy by raising crucial questions that could affect the business's future strategic health. "More than anything," says one CEO, "I want my board to help me think about strategies for survival and growth of the organization. That is the number one concern I have for the company."

Directors can play several roles in the strategy arena, including:

- Ensuring the clear articulation of strategic direction
- Reviewing the assumptions and feasibility of the strategic plan

- Providing guidance on the planning process
- Providing input on key strategic decisions, such as entry of new markets, acquisitions, or major capital investments
- Ensuring plans are implemented and revised as necessary

Overseeing Plan Development

When presented with a strategic plan, the effective director will likely contemplate one overriding question: How good is it? Every strategic plan should identify the company's business objectives, its product or service, its market scope, and its requirements for success. The work of developing this strategic plan is management's responsibility.

Yet, the effective director will work with the CEO to examine the assumptions and process that underlie the plan. Together, they can examine the plan's internal consistency and its likely effect on employees and other constituencies. They can evaluate the quality of information that went into the plan. And they can determine whether the plan is consistent with the business's overall mission and philosophy.

Ensuring the Validity of the Plan

Once completed, the board can help ensure the plan has been thought through and does not harbor any strategic contradictions. For instance, if positioning the company as a top-quality, high-priced producer is a major goal, selling surplus production through a discount retailer or warehouse club doesn't make good sense. Directors might not only spot such inconsistencies but also help come up with a more consistent (but equally efficient) idea to dispose of the surplus products.

Inconsistencies can crop up in almost every area. If part of a company's strategy is to develop teamwork among salespeople, it makes little sense to base their compensation and incentive plan solely on individual performance. While such inconsistencies may seem obvious, they can be difficult to spot amid the day-to-day pressures of running a business.

Evaluating the Strategic Planning Process

In some cases, a CEO intent on preparing a strategic plan can lose sight of the quality of the process. Yet the process can have a profound effect on the plan.

As objective outsiders with special insight into the CEO, directors can evaluate the dynamics of the process by raising some important questions. Was the process "top-down" or "bottom-up"? What questions did you ask? To whom and how did you present them? What kinds of responses did you receive?

A CEO who tries to accommodate everyone in a group planning effort may end up with a document so diluted that it is meaningless. On the other hand, a particularly strong-willed and powerful CEO may be unaware of the chilling effect of his or her personality on debate and questioning by managers. The result may be an incomplete or ill-founded document.

Ensuring the Plan is Driven by Sound Information

Another major issue is the quality of the information used in preparing the strategic plan. No matter how much inspiration and clever thinking goes into a plan, the final result is no better than the quality of the authors' information about the marketplace.

Effective directors will raise several questions:

- *"Do we understand our market share?"* Concrete market share data is crucial, not only in making realistic forecasts but in anticipating competitors' behavior.

- *"How strong is our competitive advantage?"* Going beyond broad assumptions to measure perceived advantage or quality relative to one's competitors is crucial to effective planning. The board can hold management accountable by asking all the hard questions about the company's genuine strengths and weaknesses. Understanding one's weakness in the marketplace can produce more realistic goals. And knowledge of one's strengths can help the company focus on making the most of them.

- *"How well do we know the competition?"* Any good strategic plan should acknowledge the role of competitors—their relative strength, their apparent strategy and, especially, their likely next move. The board can play an important role in ensuring the evaluation of the competitive situation of the business in the market is as thorough as it needs to be. In the case of one family business, the new independent directors asked for a thorough overview of the competition as part of their orientation to the business.

- *"How productive is our company?"* A company's actual financial performance can be obscured in many ways. Inflation, price increases, raw material price swings, and a variety of other factors can mask real results. Many senior managers are not fully aware of the message conveyed by their financial statements, and their strategic planning is blurred as a result. If sales are up 7 percent after an 8 percent price increase, management should hardly be complacent about the company's prospects. A board can help spot these aberrations and help management see what is really happening.

Ensuring the Plan is Achievable

Many strategic plans look great on paper but never progress much further than that. Once the senior management team has performed the Herculean task of completing a strategic plan, the board can help them translate it into action. What are early milestones that measure progress? Who will actually implement the plan? How will they be held accountable for implementation? What money is available to accomplish it? What's a reasonable schedule to implement this plan? By addressing these issues, management can ensure a viable plan rather than one that gathers dust in the corporate files.

Encouraging Strategic Thinking

Strategic thinking goes beyond putting a plan document together. While a sound plan is an invaluable basis for progress, strategic thinking is much more: It is a mindset, a way of thinking about the business to constantly prepare it for the future. Directors can provide invaluable support and discipline in this effort by raising crucial strategic issues.

Performance Versus Potential: How to Close the Gap?

Many family-owned businesses are undermined by a common strategic weakness: a tendency to undershoot their potential. Entrepreneurs may become reluctant to assume greater risk or to jeopardize any personal control when their companies grow established and successful. Once these hardworking CEOs have something to lose, they begin to enjoy a new sense of security. They may resist mounting new ventures that require increased borrowing, collaborating with other organizations, or bringing in a financial partner. Such snowballing conservatism can lock a promising young company in a strategic straightjacket, leaving it timid, underleveraged, and stagnant.

The boardroom is the ideal place to dissect these fears and reservations, examine their merit, and explore alternative routes to growth. Often, directors can suggest creative solutions to apparent strategic dilemmas. Other times, they can bolster CEOs' confidence in their own instincts, encouraging bold new initiatives.

Are We Looking for Growth or a Good Return?

Some companies must focus on short-term returns to service debt, satisfy lenders or ensure consistent shareholder distributions. However, many have the luxury of trading short-term profits to invest in longer-term returns. As a result, they face the ongoing challenge of deciding whether to constrain growth by taking money out of the business or to invest in new opportunities? One CEO says, "My directors ask me questions like, 'Are you committed to growth or profit? When push comes to shove, are you willing to invest to grow your market or are you trying to eke every dollar out of what you already have, by cutting back on new product development or continually raising prices?'" For now, he has decided that "investing in the market is good business. The market is growing." But if circumstances change, he adds, his perspective might shift as well.

What is Our Cost of Capital?

The family business CEO has an inherent conflict of interest on this question. The chief executive's goal should be to seek the lowest possible cost of capital (a term used to refer to the cost of money needed to grow the business—either debt or equity; the cost of debt capital is the interest rate the bank charges; the cost of equity capital is the rate of return that owners expect to receive). Managing the cost of capital requires, at least in part, holding down dividends to shareholders to reserve cash generated by the business for growth opportunities.

But maximizing the return to shareholders should also be a goal, and its one that often conflicts with minimizing the cost of capital. If shareholders press for increased quarterly dividends, the company can lose the ability to fund growth through internal cash flow and may have to resort to bank debt.

The board can help the CEO probe his or her position on this issue and examine the potential consequences of alternative positions. If shareholders are denied attractive returns for a long time, they may cause an upheaval by selling out. On the other hand, the opposite policy may leave the company stagnant and drifting. Whatever the balance, the issue is a real one.

Are We Maximizing the Value of the Business?

The board can also ensure the CEO takes the cost of capital into account in decision making with regard to major investments. If the CEO proposes investments whose returns are below the cost of capital, they will decrease the value of the firm.

Many business owners feel that placing a financial value on the business is a first step toward selling the company. In fact, the value of the business should be a constant and central yardstick for management performance. Management should continually be concerned about whether it is performing well enough to increase shareholder value over the long term.

In many small and medium-sized firms, the board can help determine the approximate shareholder value of the business. Unlike other measures, such as the current stock price or dividend yield, shareholder value reflects the present value of future cash flows. Essentially, it measures the current value of the business's future earnings when discounted to reflect the company's cost of capital.

The power of this financial measure lies in its focus on future earnings and investments and on the continuing return from the company's current investments. As a result, monitoring shareholder value automatically imposes a valuable management discipline: It forces a continual reappraisal of the performance of various investments. It requires management to do more than talk about making investments for the future—it requires a demonstration that they are paying off. Once a disciplined focus on value is in place, directors can ask questions about how shareholder value can be increased.

What is the Risk Profile of the Business?

Every entrepreneur is born with a propensity for risk taking. In the early stages of his or her business, there is usually little need to analyze it; the entrepreneur leads the organization by a combination of courage and instinct, seizing opportunities as they present themselves.

But as the company and its workforce grow, so too does management's need to understand its risk-taking posture and philosophy. Although the entrepreneur may still not even be conscious of his or her propensity for risk, that personal trait can color almost every major decision—acquisitions, the hiring of a top officer, the treatment of a new product idea. It becomes a major aspect of the corporate culture and can have a profound effect on strategy and its implementations.

An active board can help the company address this issue consciously, usually through probing questions. "What new risks are we taking?" directors may ask. "How much risk do we want to take? What is our attitude toward risk taking? How do we monitor it within the corporation? How should the company's risk-taking posture be communicated to the organization? How should we prepare the organization for the kinds of risks the company will be taking?"

The role of the board is not to influence the CEO but to help identify the desirable risk-taking posture, make it explicit throughout the organization, and ensure that management does not take undue risks that may threaten the long-term viability of the company.

Are Effective Contingency Plans in Place?

Every effective corporate strategist harbors a bevy of contingency plans—answers to questions about the "what-if" events that can throw a company off course.

What if our assessment of the market's interest in our new product is wrong? What if there is a strike? What if commodity prices skyrocket? What if our competitors retaliate after we enter this new market? Worrisome issues, indeed, and the kind business owners may easily neglect in the heat of inaugurating projects, opening new markets, or just growing the business.

The board's role in raising these questions in the form of crisis planning can be invaluable in preventing surprises—something almost no business owners like. One CEO dabbling in national advertising media markets for the first time recalls helpful advice from one of his directors: "Always make the assumption that your advertising mix is wrong, and that you're going to have to fix it. You never want to get married to one program." The suggestion, he says, prepared him for some high-stakes advertising decisions that followed.

Directors also can encourage a measure of forethought and preparation that will prevent management from being caught completely off guard by a negative turn of events. Either function can be crucial to the success, and even the survival, of the company.

Do We Have the Human Resources Needed to Support Our Strategic Goals?

All business leaders are acutely aware that competent, motivated people are crucial to any plans they make. But many unconsciously neglect the need to systematically develop this resource. As one company interviewed for this book discovered, the lack of effective human-resources planning can foil the best-laid strategy. While its owners aspired to growth through acquisition, they were forced to pass up an attractive acquisition opportunity because of an internal shortage of qualified managers to oversee the expanding business.

An effective board can be invaluable in ensuring systematic and effective human-resources planning. This entails planning for succession to all positions, not just top management. It includes policies on compensation and incentives, training and development, promotion opportunities and minimum hiring requirements. It raises questions about the company's ability to attract top people, the company's position on relocating employees, and a variety of other issues that have a bearing on the business' human resources.

Many CEOs find their boards continually help them review management depth and quality in a way that no other adviser could. By confidentially tracking the progress of employees over time and helping plan incentives and learning opportunities for high-potential managers, the board can help ensure there is a management-development system that yields a manager-in-waiting every time a new opportunity opens up. In other cases, directors can provide knowledge and insight to help avert a wide range of other problems, from rapid employee turnover to sagging morale.

But, before they can take on those and other like issues, it is important the board be properly set up to function to the utmost of its ability.

6

Designing the Board

When the 14 third-generation owners of Canal Insurance decided to add independent directors to their board, they were building on an existing board composed of three owners (two of whom worked in the business), representing the three branches of the family.

Over time, it became increasingly clear to the family and company leadership that Canal would benefit from the objectivity and perspective afforded by independent board members. While adding independent directors to the mix created challenges, the expected benefits were apparent.

"We were typical of a lot of family-run companies—there was no formal budget or strategic planning process and we had people who had worked in the business for years with no job description," says Dru James, Family Council Steering Committee Chair and third-generation owner. "It was time for greater accountability." Through a process led by a search committee composed of a subset of the ownership group and supported by a family business consultant, the Greenville, S.C., based company ultimately added four independent directors to its board.

For McKee Foods, the process of establishing a board with independent directors happened a bit differently. While for years the firm had had a formal board of directors made up of family/owner executives and a few nonfamily top management, the idea of bringing in independent outside directors had been brewing for some time, according to company president, Mike McKee: "We talked about this for the better part of a decade; we even had a couple of false runs."

When the decision was made to move forward with a board, however, company officials carefully developed both the selection process and the function of the board itself to put the right people into the ideal environment. "We created a very structured approach to choosing directors," says McKee. "And, since we were so structured, it made the board that much more effective once it was in place. When we brought in the independent directors, we ceased to have nonfamily executives on the board. In reality the two—our corporate counsel and the CFO—continue to attend most of the board meetings as nonvoting advisors and have the same, if not more, influence, but they're not on the hot seat by having to vote."

Canal's and McKee's differing experiences illustrate the varied ways an independent board can come into being in a family business. In some cases, outsiders are added to an existing family board; in others, an active board that fulfills the board functions of oversight and accountability is a new concept or one that differs significantly from what might already be in place.

No matter the circumstances, the presence of independent directors will prove a powerful element in any family business board.

However, structuring a board is a challenging task, particularly daunting for a business without any prior experience with a board. In the case of an entrepreneur's establishing a board, the structure may be as simple as that person asking a set of appropriate outsiders to join the board. In the case of family businesses that involve multiple owners in one generation, or across generations, the decision needs to be made regarding how to balance owner and independent representation on the board.

Where to Begin—Deciding Who Sits on the Board

To begin planning for an independent board, the owner (or owners) should set time aside—apart from the daily routine and ringing telephone—to reflect on the most important challenges facing the company. As discussed earlier, these challenges often arise from a handful of common and compelling concerns: "We really need to put together a succession plan," owners may conclude. Or, "We need to deal with industry consolidation. If a buyer or seller comes knocking on the door, what will our response be?" Examining the strategic challenges and opportunities present in the business can guide decisions regarding who should be sitting at the board table. The goal is to create an environment where these questions can be debated by a knowledgeable set of directors.

In cases with more than one owner, one of the first jobs is to tackle the role of owners on the board. Owners may be in leadership positions in the business, working as more junior employees, or not active in the business at all. When all owners are senior managers, it is often the case that they all sit on the board, although this becomes difficult if the number involved is greater than four or five.

In situations where a large group of owner-managers sits on the board, the board often functions more as a management committee, frequently focusing on day-to-day issues while ignoring longer term strategic issues. In addition, if this is the leadership of the business, they are not well suited to creating oversight and accountability, as they would be effectively overseeing themselves. A family board involving management and nonmanagement owners can also be counterproductive, as it can serve as a place where nonmanagement owners question and critique the actions of management, often without the required skills or insight to do so. The presence of independent directors can help address these problems.

With all owners sitting on the board, another challenge comes when some owners in the business are more junior in the management structure. In this situation it can become more complicated to involve them at a board level. A good rule of thumb: If your boss is not on the board, neither should you be. One way to address this problem is to establish criteria for family members on the board. Criteria may include involvement or rank in the business, tenure with the business, and other variables.

In the case of ownership groups where a number of owners are not active in the business, a different set of challenges arise. Should preference for board seats be given to owners who are employees, since they know the business well? Or should preference be given to nonemployed owners, to ensure their interests and concerns are recognized? As businesses move down in generations, it becomes more likely that nonemployed owners will serve on the board. In our survey of family business boards, we found 40 percent of companies with active boards had nonemployed owners on the board. (See appendix 9.)

When the ownership group becomes too large for all owners to sit on the board, the owners must determine how owners will be represented. In many cases, families choose to have branches of family ownership determine board structure (i.e., in the second generation, three brothers own the business; each of these three family branches will have one representative on the board).

Board Insight

In our experience, the more a family can move toward the notion of being one family versus multiple family branches, the better the family and business are served.

Ideally, criteria for board eligibility should be established, a profile of skills and experience valued on the board created, and nominations for family seats requested.

Models vary from family to family, but the primary objective should be to ensure the board is composed of individuals who can best fulfill its responsibilities. In situations where owners and independent directors sit on the board together, the role of a family board member may be different than that of independent directors, including:

- Serving as stewards of family values
- Providing a communication link to family members
- Representing the perspective of ownership

Board Insight

It is unlikely that owner directors, particularly those not employed in the business, will possess the same level of skills and experience that independent directors bring to the table. That said, it is best to establish criteria and training for family directors in order to ensure they can function effectively on a board with independent representation.

Requirements of all directors include an ability to read and understand financial statements and sound business judgment. Criteria unique to a family director include an ability to balance disparate viewpoints of different owners, a good relationship with all owners, and strong communication skills. In larger owners groups, family directors must also have an appreciation for the fact that their duty as directors is to represent the ownership group at large, not a constituency of that group. (See appendix 3 for a sample list of family director qualifications.)

Absent criteria for family directors, a dynamic can emerge wherein the independent directors are the vocal, active board members, and family directors defer to them. While family directors should leverage the skills and experience of their independent directors, the best dynamic is for both groups to work together to ensure the business is run effectively.

The Gorski family experience provides a great example for other families in clarifying the role and responsibilities of family directors. Says family director Judi Gorski, "In our family, we have always tried to look forward to identify problems that might arise between the family and business, and develop processes to address issues before they arise." In that vein, the family decided it would be beneficial to clarify the role and responsibilities of owners, management and directors "to help those of us wearing multiple hats to understand what role we were filling at a given time."

Once they got this effort under way, they realized it would also be useful to write down the criteria valued in family directors, the role they were expected to play, and the process by which family directors were selected. In their case, the board consists of a majority of independent directors, with two family representatives as members.

The criteria for family directors include financial acumen and business knowledge, though not at the same level as independent directors. Judi Gorski emphasizes that family directors must bring more to the table than do independent directors: "Family directors have additional responsibilities beyond independent directors in representing the family. They need to understand when they should be going to the family to get consensus from the shareholders before voting. There is a sensitivity that family directors need to have."

The Role of Independent Directors in Board Structure

Once the role of ownership on the board has been determined, the ownership group must decide how to incorporate management and independent representation. This balance is often a central decision.

Many ownership groups feel uncomfortable giving majority control of the board to nonowners. Yet, they need to remember that board members serve at the request of owners—they can be unseated if the owners do not find them helpful. In our survey, the greater the proportion of independents on a board, the more that board was judged to be effective. Boards with a majority of independent directors were deemed to be the most effective in ensuring the business is well managed. (See appendix 9.)

Some families try to keep a balance between independents and owners, in which case the size of the board and number of independent directors is often determined by the requirements for how many owners will sit on the board. Unfortunately, a board greater than eight or nine members can be difficult to manage. Typically, the suggested optimal size for boards is in the six-to-nine person range. A National Association of Corporate Directors' 2007 survey placed the average at eight board members. In our survey, average board size was seven to eight directors.

Board Insight

Whatever balance seems appropriate between independent directors and others, it is never a good idea to add just one or two independent directors.

Although some business owners may be uncomfortable about adding outsiders to their board, the presence of just one or two such directors mitigates most all potential advantages. As a distinct minority, these independent directors can be a personality rather than a voice.

Owners uncomfortable with a headfirst plunge into having independent directors may create an advisory board. Here, they can receive independent input without raising concerns about giving up control, thus allowing the family to become comfortable with the value of outside perspective.

While the advisory board can provide valuable outside input, there are downsides. In difficult circumstances advisors may not feel the same level of duty or commitment, and there may be some confusion over the authority of the advisory board versus the board of directors (if a family board or management board is also functioning). For these reasons, a board of directors is more effective than a board of advisors. Our survey results demonstrate that many families are still hesitant about the power perceived in an independent board: 21 percent of survey respondents had advisory boards in place.

One final big question is who will lead the board. In many family businesses, a retired CEO serves as the chair. By contrast, some families choose to have a nonfamily, or a nonmanagement, chair to facilitate the business of the board, ensure accountability, and make clear the delineation between ownership and management roles. In some cases the board's business is facilitated by someone who is not the chair.

The Board Prospectus

Preparing a board prospectus is one of the first steps in organizing an effective board. The prospectus is a short document (two to five pages) that outlines the purpose, goals, and design of the board. It conveys the qualities and capabilities the business owners is seeking in directors, and it describes the anticipated board structure, director compensation, and time demands on members.

Like a corporate mission statement, the board prospectus should be a unique and distinctive document illuminating the personality and values of the owners, as well as the philosophy and culture of the company. (An example of an effective prospectus is located in appendix 1.)

Developing this document is useful for multiple reasons. First and foremost, it helps owners and management get on the same page about the need for a board, the role the board will play, and the skills and experience preferred in board members. The prospectus can be used to communicate this information to potential board candidates or contacts who might know attractive director prospects.

The prospectus can also be useful in communicating the role and purpose of the board to other key stakeholders, including nonactive owners, lenders, employees, customers, and others. It can be of great help in allaying doubts among key people who are unfamiliar with the board's role or who are suspicious about involving outsiders.

Contents of the Board Prospectus

1. Overview of the Company
   - Industry
   - Most important products and types of customers
   - Size (revenues, employees)
   - Nature of ownership (e.g., two brothers as founding partners, third-generation family business with 15 shareholders)

2. Board Profile
   a. Character of business
      - Stage of life cycle (e.g., rapidly growing, maturing, no longer growing)
      - Relative strengths or weaknesses
      - Strategic thrust (e.g., international presence, committed to increasing market share)
   b. Purpose(s) of the board

   Most common examples:
      - Brainstorm and examine alternative strategic directions in an industry facing maturity and intensifying competition
      - Stimulate continued professionalism of management and organizational development
      - Aid in succession process
      - Serve as counsel to spouse and/or successors in case of death of CEO
      - Encourage self-discipline and accountability for senior management
      - Counsel and support successors
      - Develop board strength to support future financing needs or public offering
   c. Board member profile
      - Desired background, personal characteristics and experience of board candidates

3. Structure of the Board
   - Number of independent directors and owners on the board
   - Number of meetings

- Time commitment
- Participation in committees or family business activities
- Amount and form of board compensation
- Director liability provisions
- Term of office

Responsibility for developing the prospectus usually falls on the owners of the business, as it is their responsibility to establish the governance structure. In some cases, prospectus development may be directed by the CEO or senior management with input from a broader ownership group. Regardless of how it is established, the board should meet the needs of both management and owners, serving as wise counsel for the business and ensuring accountability.

What Do You Want in a Board?

The prospectus should lead off with a brief introduction stating the rationale for developing a board of directors at this time and the key goals the ownership group hopes to accomplish through the board.

The introduction should be followed by a section describing the company, its size in terms of sales and employees, its relative strengths and weaknesses and, looking forward, its major strategic goals or challenges. It should convey a sense of the company's industry, competition, customers, and business model. And while the prospectus need not reveal a great deal of financial information, it should offer director candidates a clear sense of the business's scale.

The prospectus should summarize the major corporate issues the top management and/or owners may want the board to address. For example, a prospectus might highlight the need for help in dealing with changes in consumer attitudes or federal regulation. Another may emphasize the need to explore new sources of capital or to prepare for management succession.

What Expertise Are You Seeking in Directors?

The second component of the prospectus—the board profile—is often the most challenging and stimulating to prepare. This section outlines the desired criteria for board members in terms of experience, skill, and understanding.

To reach that point, most family firms find it useful to ask a series of questions. Executives typically find that trying to answer them lends new insights that can be of great help in building a board.

What is Your Industry Profile?

The first step is to examine thoroughly the driving forces in your industry. What is the nature of the competition? Is it fragmented, oligopolistic, or undergoing fundamental change? At what state of development are the industry's principal markets—are they new, maturing, or expanding internationally? What is the nature of your customers and their buying decisions?

Directors who have operated in industries with similar dynamics may be best suited to identify creative solutions to deal with challenges you face.

What is Your Strategic Profile?

This step requires a look at the company's current stance and direction in relation to its industry. What is its market share position? Where is its competitive advantage—in differentiating its product or service from others, or in operating at a lower cost? A director whose experience has been with a company or companies with a similar strategic profile will better understand how your business works and what it will take to be successful.

What Are the Keys to Success?

Based on the company's current position in the industry, what types of tasks, decisions, people, and systems are needed to ensure its success? Does prosperity depend on securing more shelf space from powerful distributors? Does the business require a more highly motivated and effective sales force? Is raising private capital crucial to expanding the company's retail brand outlets? In the case of a family company with a broad portfolio of newspaper, radio, and cable properties, one of the keys to success was innovation. Because the media space had been redefined by the Internet and availability of free content, business models were in flux. When the ownership group agreed to add independent directors to its board, a key criterion was to find directors who have worked in industries that had faced a structural change in which companies had to reinvent themselves to survive.

What Will Be the Main Sources of Future Growth?

This analysis of future challenges is a logical extension of the previous three steps. Here, the drafters identify the most promising new markets, or new products, as well as the most important threats to success, including competitive and environmental issues.

How Will the Company's Ownership Profile Affect Its Future Direction?

Many firms seek directors with some understanding of the special ownership and management issues faced by private and family businesses. To that end, it can be helpful to build an ownership profile, describing the relationships among owners, future ownership plans, and so on. How important is maintaining private ownership? How will you address the needs of the growing number of family members who are not working in the business? Basic to this step is an examination of how ownership of the company is likely to evolve in the years to come. Many business owners also include a description of their management style, culture, and personality in the prospectus.

What is the Owners' Long-term Aspiration for the Business?

Do owners wish to keep the business within the family, grow it through acquisitions, pare the ownership group, or plan to sell it sometime in the future? As the board would be expected to examine these long-term issues, it is critical to look for members who will be certain to raise these and other related topics—members who understand the business enough to contribute to important discussions and are objective enough to offer unbiased ideas and insights. In the case of one family business, the driving force behind establishing an independent board was to shepherd them through the process of deciding whether to expand the business via acquisition or to sell. They settled on one independent director who had sold his family business and two with mergers and acquisitions experience to help them through this decision.

Once the drafters have answered these questions, several critical steps in building a board become simpler. It becomes easier to identify other businesses that demand analogous skills of their executives; it is easier to reach across industry lines for directors, and easier to identify candidates who have already achieved the goals that are still only aspirations for your business. And having arrived at clarity regarding what they need from their board, business owners gain confidence in screening directors for the qualities and experience that can make the board a success.

In the case of Canal Insurance, family members knew they wanted to focus on efforts to maximize both shareholder and company value. That, says James, compelled the company to engage in fairly comprehensive introspection.

"We were forced to reflect on what we wanted to achieve as a company," she says. "We knew we wanted our management to be more data-driven, so we looked for those sorts of characteristics in the director candidates we considered."

As it turns out, by adding four independent directors to an existing board comprised of three family members, Canal also injected a fair degree of geographic diversity into the mix. The new outside directors came from all over North America.

"We didn't set out to do it that way," James adds, "but, as we went along and since we were most interested in the skill sets that made up our board profile, we began to see some advantages to more diversity."

What Personal Qualities Do You Want in Directors?

Once the strategic profile is complete, you will also want to identify some personal criteria for directors. While some desirable qualities may seem obvious, they nevertheless bear some thought before the business owners begin the screening process. Such simple criteria as integrity and courage of conviction can be crucial to a board's success. A desire to learn is an especially appealing trait in directors, as is a strong "team player" instinct. Confidentiality, discretion, and tact often show up on this list as well.

Other dimensions, such as entrepreneurial initiative, may be inherent traits that have been enriched by experience. "A person who has spent his whole career at a company like General Motors usually has no sense of what it means to be running a $100 million firm," says one experienced director.

In particular, as family-owned businesses, you might also seek people who have shown they can sustain a successful family business, or those who have thrived in sibling partnerships. Others might look for directors who are active in political, civic, and social affairs, or who have accumulated significant personal wealth. Experience with wealth can yield valuable lessons as well as comfort for business owners seeking candidates with a similar outlook.

Finally, it is important that prospective directors appreciate the unique attributes of family businesses. Absent this characteristic, any would-be director, no matter how qualified in other respects, might simply fail to contribute as much as would a director with an affinity for family-run operations.

How Will the Board Be Structured?

The third section of the board prospectus should describe your plan for managing and structuring the board. This should be presented in enough detail that candidates will know what will be expected of them if they make a commitment to join the board. This section should outline the structure of the board, members' compensation, expected time demands, coverage for director liability, and so on.

Terms of Service

Our research indicates that few boards have stipulated terms of service. In our survey, only 6 percent of respondents with an active board had term limits, which set a maximum number of years a board member may serve (appendix 9). Term limits are used to mandate periodic change in board membership, which ensures new blood, new ideas, and a fresh perspective. In other words, it can help keep a board from becoming stale or stagnant. Additionally, terms of office induce the chair or owning family to review director performance periodically.

The downside to establishing terms of service is that they can cause effective directors to leave before management or owners want to lose them.

The goal in structuring board terms should be to maintain both freshness and stability. On one hand, the board needs to remain vital, relevant, and responsive to the changing needs of the company. On the other hand, board structure should also afford directors an opportunity to gain a long-term perspective on the business and a deep acquaintance with its owners and their values, temperament, and goals.

In the board prospectus the structure of terms should be made clear to director candidates. Neither reelection nor rotation should be automatic at the end of the term. Candidates should understand that the needs of the business may change, and that the owners may eventually need to bring in new members to reflect changing strategy, business issues, or ownership goals or characteristics.

A similar challenge is presented in establishing a mandatory retirement age for directors. On the plus side, a mandatory retirement age, often set between 65 and 70 years of age, allows for a graceful change. On the other, age does not equate with lack of involvement or insight—again, the board may inadvertently lose the services of an energetic and insightful director, age notwithstanding. Similar to our findings on term limits, our survey showed only 11 percent of active boards have a mandatory retirement age.

While mandatory director rotation enforced by term limits or retirement age can be used to ensure a well-functioning, active, and involved board, a superior approach is to develop a robust board-evaluation process. This process will ensure that problems in board function and individual director contribution are identified and addressed.

Use of Committees

One final recommendation with regard to structure is to consider the use of committees. Committees can help some boards work more effectively and efficiently by delegating some work to a smaller group. Occasionally, committees can also serve to segregate difficult decisions from owners on delicate yet important issues such as compensation and performance evaluation of family management.

Audit and compensation are the most common committees. In our survey, 24 percent of respondents with active boards had an audit committee, and 27 percent a compensation/human resources committee. (See appendix 2 for sample committee charters, outlining typical committee role and responsibilities.)

However, do not look for committees to take up business that should rightly come before the entire board. It is best that issues such as strategy, financing, and other broad-ranging topics remain the purview of the entire board so that all perspectives are considered equally.

Finally, it should be noted that while committees are an effective way to segregate specific tasks of the board, committees should not be empowered to make decisions on behalf of the board. The committee's responsibility should be to make recommendations to the full board for approval. The noted exception is an executive committee, which may be empowered in corporate bylaws to make operating decisions on behalf of the full board between board meetings. But if the board is small and readily in touch through conference calls, executive committees are not recommended. Too often, executive committees make other directors feel preempted on important matters.

What About a Transition Period?

Some companies prefer to add independent directors to their boards gradually, over a transition period of two to three years. This is particularly helpful in cases where shareholders currently serve as directors. During the establishment of an active independent board, retaining shareholders' trust and confidence in directors is crucial to avoid creating the perception that they have been forced out or shunted aside. A gradual phase-in process that permits shareholders to interact with, and gain confidence in, independent directors can be the difference between success and failure.

If the presence of management directors is at issue, the solution may be different. If the management director is near retirement age, the owners might choose to let this individual remain on the board until that time.

In most cases, though, it is better to tackle the issue directly. Once owners have made the commitment to more formal governance incorporating outside influence, this decision can be used as the catalyst for a full revamping of the board structure, including restructuring of management and ownership roles on the board. This approach ensures that independent directors can be most effective, and that all parties involved clearly understand and buy into the new structure. It also allows for the new board members to get to know each other as group and to learn together.

Scheduling Meetings

How Many Meetings?

Our research indicates that companies typically hold three or four board meetings a year, which meets the needs of most family firms. Issues seem to arise often enough that quarterly meetings are practical. At the same time, the three-month gap gives management a break from board preparation without risking that board issues lapse into inertia. Many companies have moved to adding an extra meeting each year, in the form of a strategy retreat or offsite meeting, in which board and management can dedicate focused time to the business's long-term direction. This is often a valued addition, as boards frequently find the constraint of half-day or even full-day board meetings cannot accommodate in-depth strategic discussion.

As a rule, boards should not plan to meet more than five times a year. Beyond that, directors' discussions tend to overreach into operating matters, which are management's turf. At the opposite extreme, holding fewer than three meetings allows board matters to drift too long and can prevent sufficient oversight.

Many companies have an average of one additional, unscheduled, meeting each year. Acquisition opportunities and other major business questions that arise without warning may warrant special meetings. However, boards should be cautious about calling too many unscheduled sessions. More than one special meeting a year is a signal that the management may be depending too much on the board in everyday decision making.

In planning the board calendar the chair should remember that additional events such as plant dedications, employee picnics, lunches, and other gatherings can add to the demands on the directors' time during the year. Effective directors typically spend about a half-day preparing for each meeting from materials provided by the chair, and often are on call informally for another few hours each quarter. The board commitment adds up to an average of two to three days of time required each quarter, or an average of about eight to twelve days a year, in a steady-state environment.

If an acquisition or other major strategic decision arises, the time commitment can expand dramatically. Any committees the board forms will further increase the time requirements. All these factors weigh in favor of holding down the number of regularly scheduled board meetings to four or five per year.

How Should Meetings Be Structured?

Board meetings typically should run about four to six hours. Most boards cannot accomplish all they need to in less time. At the same time, most groups grow less effective in meetings of more than five hours. The National Association of Corporate Directors puts the average meeting length at five-and-a-half hours.

However, it is important to stress that the length of meetings depends in part upon the complexity and size of the business. For instance, if a business consists of multiple business units, or the board is large, with a number of committees, meetings can be long. One strategy to offset this is to schedule committee meetings on the day prior to the board meeting.

The morning time slot—from 8:30 a.m. until 12:30 p.m., for instance—is often best for directors, who are used to kicking off their workday first thing. Many companies serve a light buffet lunch afterward. Managers or family shareholders are often invited to join in these informal meals, a gesture that helps build trust and rapport with directors. If directors have to travel from out of town, some boards also elect to hold informal meals the night prior to the board meeting, giving independent directors time for themselves or to meet with family owners.

Another important courtesy is to set a departure time and stick to it. If you promise directors will be free to leave by 1 p.m., they should be able to count on that.

Compensating Directors

The amount of compensation should be included in the board prospectus, enabling prospective directors to know exactly what remuneration will be involved in any invitation to serve.

In setting director compensation for the first time, owners should begin with the assumption that they cannot pay qualified directors what they are genuinely worth. Often, directors come from bigger companies and have already achieved the goals the management and owners are hoping to attain. Most are busy people with abundant other demands on their time.

The compensation should be set to show that the owners appreciate the contribution made by the directors. The fee should roughly reflect the time the director is expected to devote to the company, at a rate similar to what the firm pays the CEO in salary for comparable time (i.e., divide CEO annual compensation by 240–250 working days per year for a daily rate, then multiply by eight to 12 days per year). Compensation should be high enough that it reflects a significant commitment to the board on the part of the owners—an investment in the company's future. It also should be generous enough that the chair will not feel guilty making occasional extra demands on the director's time—to attend a plant opening or strategic planning meeting, for instance. Owners should consider that for some directors, your board opportunity will be one of many. When directors have served on public company boards, their compensation expectations may be significantly higher.

There are several ways to pay directors, including combinations of per-meeting fees and annual retainers. An ideal scenario is an annual retainer (paid in quarterly installments) and a per-meeting fee. The NACD reports an average of $2,500 fee per meeting with an average $25,000 retainer, leading to a total average annual compensation of $35,000 for a board member. In our survey, for those companies who reported compensation, 32 percent paid a retainer only, 44 percent paid meeting fees only and 18 percent paid both (see appendix 9). Additionally, the NACD estimates an additional $1,500 per meeting on average for committee work.

The NACD also reports incentive compensation tied to stock options or grants; however, family businesses typically do not wish to give ownership or equity incentives to directors. In our survey, 8 percent of those reporting compensation paid some type of incentive compensation, either stock-based or other.

It is important to note that these are average figures, and that compensation varies considerably. In our survey, we found no clear pattern in compensation, other than that it generally increases according to the size of the business and the amount of time a director must commit.

Some owners question whether directors should be paid if they do not attend a meeting. The simple answer is, yes. While some owners think directors need a financial incentive to come to meetings, remuneration is typically the furthest thing from the mind of a capable board member. Rather, the chair should try to underscore the director's role as a consistent resource to the company. This attitude will usually yield rich rewards, encouraging directors to take a sustained interest in the company and to make themselves available to help in a variety of ways.

How does a per-meeting fee differ from a retainer paid quarterly? The only real difference is that additional per-meeting fees should be paid if more meetings are added to the schedule. This structure serves to encourage the company to call extra meetings should an unusual situation arise in which additional meetings are warranted. Some boards elect to pay only for face-to-face meetings. However, if telephonic meetings extend beyond two hours, they should be considered compensated meetings.

Most small and medium-sized private companies handle directors' compensation as cash payments. Some, however, set up for directors a deferred-compensation plan enabling them to receive their fees at a specified future date. Often, this enables directors to defer income until after retirement.

No matter how generous the compensation, it is difficult to pay motivated and involved directors adequately for all they can bring to a family-owned business. Rather, compensation should be viewed as an expression of appreciation for directors' time and effort.

Now that we have clarified how to determine what you are looking for in directors and in the structure and function of the board, it is appropriate to turn our attention to finding and selecting the directors who best fit the needs of your business.

Finding and Selecting Directors

One of the most challenging and rewarding dimensions of building an independent board is finding and selecting independent directors. The ultimate goal is to assemble a group with a wellspring of experience relevant to the business's needs and who share a sincere interest in the welfare of the owning family and all the firm's constituents.

Once a board prospectus is developed, it is time to seek out candidates for the board.

The process is much like hiring an important employee. "The whole key is getting what you need, just as if you were a manager filling the weak spots in your division with quality people," says one business owner.

This chapter is designed for the ownership group that has reached this stage, to help them understand and manage this process. It offers guidance on whom to consider for the board. It describes some subtleties of the search, including: the role a large ownership group may play in the process, ensuring diversity among directors, and dealing with fears of rejection or error. It also discusses how to approach candidates and make selections.

Beginning Your Search

"Whom do we leave off?" is the first question many family business owners ask in establishing an active independent board. "How can we possibly include all the deserving candidates—our customers, trusted friends, banker, accountant, lawyer, vice-president for sales, joint-venture partners, minority investors?"

The answer: Leave them all off.

Politics, bolstering egos, conveying thanks, rewarding performance, satisfying interest groups—ideally, none of these factors should play a role in selecting directors. Instead, the CEO, chairman, and ownership group should design the board to fulfill two purposes: to meet the needs of the company and the owners, and to support the needs of the business's leadership.

Let us look at the strengths and weaknesses of various kinds of outside board candidates:

Paid Advisers

Paid advisers are inappropriate candidates. The services of these professionals—which can include attorneys, accountants, financial planners, and others—are already available, and they bring an inherent conflict of interest to the boardroom. For one thing, they can be put in the awkward situation of making recommendations that benefit themselves directly; moreover, they may also be less willing to question the CEO if they feel they could lose the company's business.

Some owners find it pays to make exceptions for advisers not employed by the business who have broad exposure to top executives of a wide range of businesses. These professionals often develop executive skills and can be a valuable resource, even if they lack experience in starting or running a company. However, advisers who are being paid by the company should never be considered.

Friends

Trusted friends are not good choices as directors, either. Friends are harder to find than directors, and their advice and counsel are usually freely available anyway. Why jeopardize a good friendship by subjecting it to the stresses of the boardroom?

One owner faced a dilemma after naming a longtime family friend to her board. When she asked the director to step down after several years to permit her to bring some fresh perspective to the board, the director called her the next day.

"Janet, I couldn't sleep last night. I was hurt," the director told her. "I've been with the family all these years. Do you mind if I sit in the back of the room at the board meetings and just listen?" This awkward and painful situation led the CEO, against her better judgment, to retain the director.

Further, personal friends of the CEO, or chairman, or head of the search committee will likely raise questions or concerns with other family owners over conflict of interest—even if these directors can be objective, they may be seen as biased.

Retirees

Another common temptation is to focus on retirees as candidates. After all, retirees are highly visible, often available, and have abundant experience. But, while retirees can be excellent directors, they do carry possible downsides. One risk is that those who have been retired for several years may not be as current with regard to ongoing business trends as other potential candidates might be.

Another is that directorships can become too important to the retiree. If holding seats on corporate boards is a major source of ego support and stimulation, retirees can become so protective of losing the directorships that they grow too timid and too eager to please. This compromises the independent contribution the retiree might otherwise make and amounts essentially to a conflict of interest.

On the other hand, sitting executives often have far greater time constraints running their own businesses. That can make recent retirees a very attractive choice. Recently retired executives, who are very much in step with current business conditions and practices and with sufficient time to devote to the board, make good potential candidates. When considering retirees as candidates, look closely at what is keeping them intellectually and strategically engaged and fresh. Also consider whether they will remain so for five or more years.

Academics

Owners should be equally cautious about including representatives of nonprofit institutions. In some cases, people from universities, schools, charities, think tanks or other organizations can be excellent directors. Arguably, they may also be more available than corporate CEOs. Nevertheless, performance-driven business owners run a risk in enlisting someone without experience in a profit-making organization and a background in leading people and enterprises.

People Who Hold Multiple Directorships

Candidates who already serve on several boards are risky recruits. First, they may lack sufficient time. Additionally, as they have already gained directorial experience elsewhere, they may not see joining your board as great a benefit from a learning perspective. It is also a good idea to avoid a candidate who is simply in it for the money.

That said, it is valuable to find someone who understands the role of the director. That makes prior director experience important. Moreover, serving on one or two other boards is not necessarily prohibitive. Just make sure any candidate has the right motivation for serving and has the necessary time available.

Division Heads

Heads of functional areas (e.g., marketing or human resources) or subsidiaries of larger companies can be good directors. But it is important that the individuals under-stand all the aspects of a business, not just a subset. On the other hand, depending upon the strategic challenges facing the company, it can be advantageous to look for one indi-vidual with a strong background in a particular area, such as marketing or finance. CFOs are often viewed as strong board candidates, particularly those who have good strategic as well as financial insight. In general, an individual who is a strong general manager, with knowledge of finance, market-ing, operations, and other issues is the best choice.

Other CEOs, Entrepreneurs, and Business Owners

"Risk-taking peers," in the words of Leon Danco, a pioneer family business consultant, often make the best directors.

Board Insight

People from larger, privately controlled companies who have weathered the crises or surmounted the hurdles that still lie ahead for you are the best candidates of all.

These candidates bring to the boardroom none of the con-flicts of interest or weaknesses associated with other kinds of candidates. More importantly, they offer unparalleled con-temporary experience, perspective, and empathy for govern-ing a business.

However, one should avoid those who have any overlap-ping directorships, meaning those who sit on another board with one of your directors. Overlapping directorships risk compromising the director's independence and creating an incestuous situation. If directors have another relationship in the back of their minds, they may temper their decisions and comments to protect the other relationship.

There is one final issue to be aware of with CEO directors—it takes a special mindset to be a director. Directors ask good questions, raise concerns, and offer insights. They are collegial. They are not in charge. Some CEOs have a difficult time adjusting their mindsets from running the show to providing oversight and counsel. It is crucial that all directors understand their roles and responsibilities to avoid this problem.

Aim High

Above all, owners should set high standards in the search for directors, seeking out the very best people to be found. "Our independent directors brought a lot of professionalism to the company," says Murray Berstein of Nixon Uniform. "They helped us identify niches that were simply not profitable. With the right directors, you're receiving valuable input from day one."

To illustrate: One company owner with a generous employee stock-purchase plan did not feel he was reaping the potential benefits associated with employee ownership, so he sought out as a director another CEO with a long and successful track record with such plans.

Another family business was contemplating the eventual sale of the company. They named two directors who had already started, then sold, their companies. Still another company wanted to explore joint ventures and acquisitions. For help, they sought out as a director an entrepreneur who had sold the family's commodity-foods business for $100 million and reinvested in several successful new ventures with strong growth prospects. Now the director is helping the company identify targets for investment or acquisition.

In general, the goal is to find directors whose experience relates to the specific challenges or opportunities at hand and/or whose businesses or industries are similarly structured. Examples of strategic challenges or opportunities include growth through acquisition, launching a new

product or service, and overseas expansion. Industry structure variables to be considered include, among others: degree
of capital intensiveness; whether your product or service is a
commodity or demands a premium in the market; the level
of competition you face; and degree of reliance on key suppliers. The more experience your directors have in analogous
environments with similar strategic issues, the more relevant
their advice will be.

Who Participates in the Search Process?

It is important to clarify at the start of the process the people
responsible for identifying candidates, for meeting them, and
finally for selecting those to stand for election. For first- or
second-generation companies, in which all the owners may
be involved in senior management, the search process can be
led by senior management. In some cases, the responsibility for identifying candidates may rest with the owner CEO.
However, when companies move down in generations, it is
important to determine the balance of participation between
owners in management versus nonemployed owners. In situations where a board already includes independent representation, the search for new directors may be led by a nominating
committee of the board. In some cases, this committee will
include input from the broader shareholder group. (This
topic is discussed in chapter 10, where we highlight special
situations related to more mature ownership groups.)

One option for leading a first-time search is a formal committee. As we move through this chapter, the individual or
individuals responsible for identifying candidates will be
referred to as the "search committee." Canal Insurance used
this strategy to put together its board of directors. The ownership group of Canal selected three representatives to oversee the
search process—one from each of three ownership branches.
Although Canal's committee by design did not include
executives—the ownership group felt the board movement
should be led and championed by owners—the committee

led the development of a prospectus with input from both owners and management. From there, the committee worked with a family business consultant to identify candidates.

After the consultant conducted an initial set of screening interviews, the search committee conducted more in-depth interviews and narrowed the list to a recommended few candidates. The search committee understood that management would have a good sense of the skills and experience needed on the board, so it invited management to participate in interviews even though they did not have a vote in the actual selection process.

In larger ownership groups, deciding who will serve on the search committee is an important step in the overall search process. One option is for the owners to elect a search committee in a special family meeting or through the family council (if there is one). Another option is to set the committee up to reflect the makeup of the ownership group—either by generation or family unit. Ideally, search-committee members should be individuals who understand the role and responsibilities of a board, do not have particular biases toward management or a subset of owners, and who will do a good job of representing the family business to candidates.

Families differ in their consideration of how management should be represented on the search committee. Often management will have the best sense of the skills and experience that would be most beneficial in the boardroom. So, if there is not direct management participation in the committee, they should still be involved in the interview process.

For cases in which the search committee involves a subset of owners, it is important to keep the other owners informed as the process moves along. The ownership group should have an opportunity to provide input to the board prospectus. In one successful search process, all owners were interviewed by the family business consultant and reviewed the prospectus draft before it was finalized. In addition, owners received email updates on the progress of the search as each set of interviews was completed. Finally, prior to the election process, the search committee sent a formal memo to owners summarizing the backgrounds of the candidates it recommended for election and the rationale for their selection. Prior to the board election, this information was reviewed in a family meeting in which family members had an opportunity to ask questions of the search committee.

One important subtlety to keep in mind is that those on the committee responsible for the search do not necessarily have the final authority to elect directors. The responsibility of the search committee is to identify good candidates and make recommendations to shareholders, who have the legal authority to elect directors to the board.

How Do We Find Candidates?

One of the best ways to begin networking for board candidates is to ask for suggestions from all those people not considered for the board.

Customers, suppliers, friends, bankers, lawyers, accountants, and consultants can all be valuable sources of referrals. A letter with the prospectus enclosed is a good way to ask for help. (See appendix 4 for introductory letter.)

Members of professional associations can be helpful as well, including the Young Presidents Association, chapters of Vistage, and other CEO groups. The National Association of Corporate Directors in Washington, D.C., also maintains a list of director candidates, which is available to its members.

Tapping into family business networks, such as college- and university-based family business programs, can be a wonderful resource to identify fellow business owners. Family business consultants can also be a great resource in identifying candidates.

Using a Search Firm or Other Outside Support

Search firms can be helpful, and some conduct director searches regularly. The search committee should be prepared to pay the equivalent of one year of an individual director's fees for the service.

Some owners value search firms because they can act as third-party recruiters, making it less awkward for either the candidate or the search committee to break off discussions if one party is not interested.

In practice, however, search firms are rarely used to find private company directors. In our survey of family business boards, 19 percent of those with independent directors reported using a search firm. Of those, 69 percent came from businesses of $250 million or larger in revenue, and 54 percent from businesses in the fourth generation or beyond. In the same survey, three-quarters of those with independent directors reported knowing the director prior to placing the individual on the board. On the one hand, this may suggest that company owners have a habit of putting their friends or advisors on their board. On the other, it implies that owners are simply more comfortable approaching people they already know. Both these tendencies reinforce the value of using a search firm that is sensitive to the needs of family-owned businesses.

Beyond search firms, there are other outside resources that may be used to identify directors. In particular, family business consultants may play the role of assisting in constructing an independent board. A family business consultant provides an added benefit beyond a search firm in that they can work with the family members to educate them on the role and value of the board, can facilitate gaining consensus among owners around the need for and uses of a board, and can advise on the appropriate board structure needed to support the business and its ownership group. In addition, family business consultants will typically have a broad range of contacts from other family businesses who may be suitable board candidates.

Subtleties of the Search

No matter how carefully the search committee may have considered the criteria for directors listed in the board prospectus, some additional and more subtle criteria may warrant thought at this stage.

The Age Factor

Some family firms or search committees seek a particular age distribution on the board. Those who have chosen a successor like to have at least one director who is of a comparable age, as well as directors of other ages to lend freshness, perspective, and continuity to a board.

One first-generation business owner constructed his board to bridge the "generation gap" between himself and the next generation of managers in his company. Among his three independent directors, one is a male about the owner's age with accounting, marketing, and family business expertise. Another is the young female CFO of a family business. The third is the CEO of a larger, family-owned wholesale distribution firm in another industry who in age is between the owner-manager and his children. His children were deeply involved in selecting directors and had veto power over his choices.

The board members also provide a philosophical bridge. The business owner intentionally selected directors he believes will be more progressive than he is. He thinks their philosophies will harmonize better with his children's. "The board really is the kids' board," he says.

Gender and Cultural Representations

Some search committees seek directors who mirror the gender and cultural patterns of their shareholders or employees or customers. This composition ensures different perspectives are represented on the board.

It also makes a statement about corporate identity and values, sending a signal that the company values diversity and will give power to socially less enfranchised groups.

For instance, a service firm with a large number of professional female employees might seek two or more women directors with similar backgrounds. But family firms should be aware of the risk of unwittingly creating a constituency board, in which individual directors feel an overriding loyalty to certain shareholders, employee groups, or other constituents.

If the head of a family business places an experienced family business owner on the board, there is a risk that family members will seek out that person as their special representative. In such cases, the director should be perceptive and strong-minded enough to stress his or her attentiveness to the interests of all shareholders, and to the company as a whole.

The U.S. Senate provides a usefully analogy. Like senators elected at large from each of the 50 states, the director's duty is to represent the interests of all corporate shareholders at large—not of interest groups, family branches, individual, or other constituencies within the company.

Covering Crucial Areas of Expertise

Striking a balance among directors with various backgrounds is another subtle but important factor in building an effective board.

If the search committee has identified one or more crucial areas of expertise for directors, such as marketing or research and development, they should probably recruit at least two people with some expertise in that area. That provides an insurance policy that all or most aspects of the field will be covered and that some expert input will be available at every board meeting. For a business that is looking to expand overseas, the search committee might want to identify two of the three to five outside directors as having international expertise.

But, the search committee should avoid overloading the board with people of similar backgrounds. The goal should be to assemble a group with complementary, not equivalent, experience.

"A board that functions well usually has people with complementary professional skills," says an experienced director. "The directors shouldn't all be in the same profession and competing with each other to be the most brilliant person in the field."

Help for the CEO Lacking Board Experience

> ### Board Insight
> When the CEO or board chair of the family firm lacks experience with an independent board, the search committee might consider recruiting one person as a kind of facilitator or board manager, particularly in the first few years of the board's operation.

The board faciliator may or may not be a voting director but should have broad experience with board operations, a working knowledge of board management details, and an ability to tactfully and discreetly guide both the chairman and the directors toward the common goal of a well-functioning board. This is akin to the "lead director" concept in publicly held companies.

Another option is naming an independent director as chair of the board, a concept covered in chapter 8.

The Importance of Board Experience for Directors

People who have served on other boards, or who have outside boards of their own, are often the best director candidates. Ideally, at least two directors will have such experience, particularly in cases where the CEO or chairman does not have board experience. The search committee should also seek people with at least some experience on the boards of profit-making organizations. A background with the boards of nonprofit organizations or financial institutions is often less helpful, as discussed earlier. Another interesting category to consider is nonemployed owners of other family businesses who sit on their boards. They can bring a unique ownership perspective to the mix.

Dealing with Fears of Rejection or Mistakes

Any search committee approaching truly worthy board candidates is almost certain to have some qualms. "Why would these top-flight people want to serve on *our* board?" they may wonder. "What if we ask someone who says no? Or, what if we decide that we don't want to choose someone who is very interested in serving?"

In practice, rejection by a candidate who has shown interest through the search process is not very likely. As discussed earlier, many people relish the opportunities afforded by the membership on an active, vital board. (This is most true of people who do not already serve on more than one board.) Very often, CEOs are eager to participate for the learning experience and enjoyment.

Most business leaders are flattered when another well-respected business approaches them and says, "Look, our business is facing these challenges over the next several years, and I know you've been successful in these areas. I think you can help us." In fact, the odds that a candidate will accept an offer of a directorship are usually much better than 50–50. Contacting candidates through mutual acquaintances or friends of friends improves those odds.

"When I was first approached to join the board, I thought I would never serve on a board of a company that small," says Randy Larrimore, a director on Nixon Uniform's board. "But I was intrigued by their professionalism and what the company was doing. I was excited about the prospect of asking questions that for many in the business were unfathomable to ask." In addition to serving on Nixon's board, Larrimore has served as a director on large, public company boards and has run a multi-billion dollar business.

Search committees may also have anxiety about how to deal with candidates whom they consider but decide not to select for the board. This concern is addressed in the next section.

How to Approach Candidates

The search committee has identified a long list of prospects. What is the next step? That depends on who is responsible for vetting the candidates:

- If it is the company CEO or board chair, they can make a call to set up a face-to-face meeting or a phone interview.
- If a search committee is in place, the chair of search committee can make the call.
- In the case of use of a consultant or search firm, the professional advisor generally makes the first call and may conduct initial interviews to screen out uninterested or unqualified candidates.

Regardless who is responsible for the search, if a candidate was recommended by a person who knows the individual, one should request an introduction through that person. Even prior to the CEO or search committee making contact, the person making the recommendation may verify the candidate's interest. And, no matter who makes contact, they should offer to send the prospectus via mail or email for the candidate to read before any interview. When the candidate is approached, either by a colleague who recommends the individual or by the search committee, the candidate should be asked to share a vita or bio with the search committee.

Those responsible for the search should be careful throughout these initial contacts to use the word "candidate" rather than "director," to avoid creating the impression among recruits that their selection is automatic. The interviewer might explain, "We're interviewing five or six people to try to find a mix of candidates whose backgrounds complement each other and serve the needs of our business. We'd like to get to know you better and give you a chance to know us. Can we have a meeting?" This approach opens a door at the outset to terminating the discussions without an offer.

A visit to the candidate's business can provide helpful insight. During the first phone call, the search committee representative might offer to meet the candidate at his or her office. If a tour is offered, accept! meetings at the candidate's office give the search committee an opportunity to experience the culture of the business, providing powerful insight into the candidate's fit with your own business. (At some point during the selection process, the candidate should visit your corporate headquarters and perhaps another major facility as well, providing insight into your business culture.) Least useful is a meeting at a neutral location, such as a restaurant, which provides no opportunity for the candidate and search committee to learn more about each others' businesses.

If a candidate is not local, the initial meeting is most often conducted over the phone. If far-flung candidates seem attractive after the initial conversation, they are brought in at the company's expense for a meeting with senior management and the search committee (if one is being used).

At the first meeting or phone conversation, the search committee should take a few minutes to introduce themselves and the company, to describe the objectives of the meeting, and, if appropriate, to explain how they came to contact the candidate. Candor can help the get-acquainted process along. "We'd like to share with you some of our thinking about the problems we face," the search committee might tell the candidate. After a summary of some issues, the search committee might ask, "How does this compare with your experience?" The response will speak volumes about the candidate's ability to provide helpful insights.

Asking questions about the candidate's own business can help put the individual at ease. The answers will help demonstrate the resources this person might offer as a director and allow you to gauge his or her candor.

Many search committees also like to use this first meeting to describe the expected role of the board in relation to the CEO. For instance, the committee might make it clear that owners do not intend to abdicate management responsibility to the board. The directors will not be held accountable or made to feel responsible for decision making, but their advice and opinions will be highly valued.

The search committee should not progress to a second meeting with the candidate unless an offer to join the board is very likely. Protracted talks followed by a "no thanks" can create hard feelings. Also, by the second meeting, the search committee should feel comfortable sharing more financial data and business details to give the candidate a clearer picture of the board issues that lie ahead. Information that should be shared in a second meeting would include: audited financial statements, the annual budget, the strategic plan (if available), information on key customers and suppliers, senior management biographies, an organization chart, corporate bylaws, the parameters of D&O (directors and officers) insurance, and any other information that will help the potential director get a good perspective on the business. In presenting this information, if there are concerns over confidentially, it is reasonable to ask director candidates to sign a nondisclosure agreement.

As discussed later in this chapter, the search committee should have cross-checked the candidate's appropriateness with at least one third party. If the CEO and other key senior management are not on the committee, the committee members should make sure these others are comfortable with the candidates. While the board's role includes oversight of management, it also serves to support management, providing counsel on critical issues. So, a good working relationship with management is crucial.

Some wonder how hard they should try to sell an attractive candidate on a directorship. It is appropriate to do some selling, partly because most candidates want to be persuaded.

The offer to serve as a director may be a foreign concept to most candidates, and you may need to help them overcome concerns about the time commitment required, their legal liability, and so on. However, the search committee should be cautious in selling the board too hard, lest they succeed in recruiting someone who truly lacks the time, interests, or commitment to do the job well. The search committee should also scrupulously avoid creating any sense among candidates that they are in competition with one another.

Board Insight

As a general rule, it is a good idea to identify about twice as many candidates as board positions to provide a good pool from which to choose.

The pool of candidates should present a range of background and experience to permit effective comparison. A large pool also ensures that if some are not available or interested, or not a good fit, there are backups readily available.

Additionally, it is wise to identify an entire pool of candidates before beginning to contact them. If candidates are contacted one at a time and some are not interested, it can take a long time to find replacements; that leaves those interested candidates sitting on their hands waiting, raising their concern about commitment to the board.

A Note on Director Liability

Liability is rightfully a concern of potential directors. In most cases, candidates will need an understanding of how they are protected from potential lawsuits by shareholders, customers, employees, and other stakeholders before they are willing to accept a director position. The more personal wealth a director has at stake, and the more experience as a director, the greater these concerns may become. These worries have become more pronounced with high-profile cases in which public company directors have been sued.

The truth is that the likelihood of a suit is extremely small. This blanket statement obviously depends on the industry; in some, the likelihood of legal action is higher. Moreover, the more uninvolved the owners, the greater the likelihood of a suit.

Two ways directors can be protected are indemnification and insurance. Corporate indemnification is by far the most common line of defense. It is a promise, contained in the corporate charter, bylaws or individual contracts to protect directors from personal liability and legal costs, barring criminal liability or negligence.

If a company fails or goes bankrupt, of course, such promises are worthless. Corporate indemnification runs only as deep as the financial resources of the company. Some businesses post surety bonds to protect directors in the event of corporate insolvency or bankruptcy.

Shareholder indemnification, although far less common than corporate indemnification, is especially effective. It entails a promise by shareholders to indemnify directors against personal liability. Presumably, this deepens the financial resources available to defend directors and shields them from shareholder actions as well.

A third option is Director and Officers Insurance (D&O). Most policies complement corporate indemnification in two ways. First, they protect the personal assets of directors and officers by insuring against any liability for which the corporation does not provide indemnification. Second, these policies also protect the company's assets by reimbursing it for payments made to indemnify officers and directors.

With respect to insurance, it is standard practice for directors to request D&O coverage. In many cases, companies already have the insurance for officers and need to add directors to the policy. Seasoned director candidates may also have input on the level of coverage they would expect. A 2005 Tillinghast survey showed that the average coverage limit for companies of $100 million or less in assets was $5 million. That increases to an average of $16.5 million for companies with $100 million to $400 million in assets. For these levels of coverage premiums are often in the $15,000 to $30,000 per year range.

Cross-checking Candidates

Checking out candidates is a crucial part of the search process. The search committee should not rely solely on a primary referral. They should seek out other individuals who know the candidate well and ask for more information before contact or interview.

The cross-checking process is one reason board selections can take a month or more. It requires identifying mutual acquaintances who have had personal or business associations with the candidates and contacting these acquaintance in an unhurried moment for a confidential talk. This is one of the most important ways to avoid mistakes in the board-selection process.

Making the Final Selections

Depending upon who is involved, the process for making final selections may differ. If a search committee is involved, it will first want input from the CEO, who may not be on the committee. The committee can then hold a meeting to review candidates against the position profile and determine who best fits. From there, it can reach out to those individuals to ensure they would like to stand for election, then present the slate to shareholders. In most cases, the slate should include the number of independent directors the owners intend to elect, not more. The election process should not be used as a way to narrow down the candidate pool. When candidates are asked to stand for election, they should be reasonably assured of election.

If there is a large shareholder group in which not all owners have been involved in the process, those in charge of the
search should provide background information on candidates, including vitae and a summary of what has been
learned in interviews. In the case of an owner, CEO, or smaller
ownership group, the process may be more informal.

With respect to how the group selecting directors should
make its final choices, the board prospectus should serve as
a guide. Beyond the hard skills and experience sought, ethics and personal chemistry must be considered. No matter
how appealing a candidate's background or experience, the
search committee should reject people if there is a concern
with regard to personality fit. Even if there is a nagging feeling that a person is not quite right—a feeling that cannot be
expressed—it is best to go with that feeling.

Candidates should show candor, an eagerness to learn,
and a lively interest in the business. They should demonstrate courage of their convictions, a readiness to say what
they believe. Candidates should also demonstrate the kind of
personality that can be effective in a boardroom setting, such
as the ability to be a team player.

Depending on the owner's tastes, desires and needs, other
qualities may figure into the final decision as well—anything
from family values or creativity to status and wealth.

Usually, the candidates who are the best fit with the skills
and experience outlined in the prospectus and the personality characteristics listed above will be obvious, and the
search committee will not have a problem reaching consensus. However, this ideal situation does not always emerge. If
the committee does not reach a consensus on the best candidates, it may need to go through an exercise to compare the
attributes of candidates. In order to compare candidates on
an even playing field, the members of the search committee
should each rate the candidates based upon a set of agreed-
upon criteria tied to the board prospectus (see appendix 5
for an example rating sheet). These ratings can be used to
facilitate conversations about candidates. By using a rating

sheet, search committee members can identify areas where they have a difference of opinion concerning a candidate.

If the group still cannot come to consensus, a vote may need to be taken. However, it is not wise to consider a candidate for whom the vote is close (four to two, for example). Remember, the candidate will need to be elected by the very shareholders on the committee who have opposed this person. However, if there is one member of the committee who does not support a candidate, the group may elect to move forward with the candidate. This individual's concerns should be shared with the full shareholder group as part of the information provided prior to an election.

How to Say No

Many search committees worry about how to say *no* to candidates who have not been selected. First and foremost, unless they are strongly interested in a candidate the search committee should be careful not to let the screening process go too far. It would be a mistake, for instance, to set up more than one meeting with a candidate or ask the individual to "meet the family" unless the prospects of becoming a director are fairly solid.

When the time comes to say *no*, the best approach is to emphasize the goal mentioned at the outset of the screening process: to select a complementary group of people with a mix of backgrounds and expertise to match the needs of the business. If the candidate does not meet the needs of the business at the moment, or complement the group you have assembled, that is no reflection on the individual's merit. The search committee might explain, for instance, that they have selected other directors because they had abilities specific to the problems the company will face in the next two to three years. One search committee told a candidate whom they had not selected that the company was focused specifically on candidates with experience in multigenerational family businesses, an area of expertise this candidate did not have.

At the same time, the search committee should express appreciation for the candidate's talents and experience, enjoyment at getting acquainted, and thanks for the time the candidate has spent.

If a search firm or family business consultant has been involved in the process, they can take responsibility for notifying candidates. However, if the search committee has developed a good relationship with a candidate through the process, it would be wise for a member of the committee to reach out to the candidate. Beyond the candidate, if a person close to the family business has recommended a candidate who is not selected, that person should be contacted regarding the outcome of the search and also the reason this candidate was not selected.

What If We Make an Inappropriate Choice?

Despite the favorable odds mentioned above, people sometimes make mistakes in selecting directors. Errors usually do not become clear immediately. It typically takes a year or two to conclude that a director simply is not making a contribution. Our experience is that this happens rarely, perhaps only one in 20 cases.

Once a mistake is discovered, it is best to act promptly. In this case, the responsibility is no longer that of the search committee but rather of the board chair (who is often the CEO) or governance committee, if one exists. Most board chairs find the best way to deal with mistakes is to approach the candidate directly and ask the person to step down. Sometimes the chair can explain to the director that the needs of the business are changing, and skills and background different from the individual's are now needed on the board.

Other times, the chair needs to say more directly: "Look we really value your contribution, but we just don't feel this is working out as we had planned, perhaps not for you also. Please understand our appreciation for all that you have done."

In other cases, boards have sought the help of professional advisers in evaluating and remaking their boards, particularly if more than one director needs to be removed.

Instituting a board-evaluation process at the time the board is launched is one way to aid in the case of a bad choice. At the end of the first year of service, the evaluation process allows the board to examine its effectiveness and determine if there are any problems with how it is being run or with the contributions of individual members. The evaluation process, which should be conducted by the chair or the governance committee, also offers an opportunity for a conversation with a member who may not be a good fit.

Getting a Board in Place in Less Than a Year

Some owners hesitate to add independent directors because the process seems complicated and time-consuming. They often worry it may take years to get a board in place. But, if a clear process is followed with a group that is given authority and accountability for spearheading the process, it can be accomplished in less than a year. Here are the steps and timing in a typical board-search process when putting together an independent board for the first time. Adding or replacing independent directors can occur even more rapidly, in as little as three months.

1. Shareholder/CEO articulates desire to add independent directors at family council meeting/management meeting (January)
2. Owners gain consensus on desire to add independent directors (February–March); this could take more time if people are not in agreement; interested parties may need to find ways to educate others on the benefit of independent directors
3. Owners identify subset responsible for search process (March)
4. Search committee develops prospectus, soliciting input from owners and management (April)

5. Owners and management confirm prospectus (May)
6. Search committee networks to identify candidates (May–June)
7. Search committee screens initial candidate list to select those with best fit, via vitae and phone interviews (July)
8. Search committee meets to narrow down list to most qualified candidates (early August)
9. Search committee contacts selected candidates to set up face-to-face interviews with committee and management (August)
10. Committee and management interview candidates (September)
11. Search committee checks references of candidates (September)
12. Search committee recommends slate to shareholders for approval (end of September)
13. Owners elect directors (October)
14. Board holds first meeting (November/December)

Case Study: Schurz Communications

Schurz Communications recently elected its first independent board members. The events that led up to their decision to reconstitute their board—consisting of owners and management—and the process used to identify directors exemplify a well-run board development process.

Schurz, a media company with radio station, cable television, and local newspaper properties in markets across the United States, is owned by the fourth and fifth generations of the Schurz family. After operating with a family and management board for several years, the family began to consider the value independent directors would add to their decision making.

The process started with the creation of a Committee on Family Governance. The committee was tasked with evaluating the family governance structure for the fifth generation and its role in Schurz Communications, and the composition of the board of directors. The scope of work grew out of the recommendations of a family business consultant who had interviewed all shareholders as part of his engagement with the family. The consultant observed that because key owner/managers had dominated the board, the fourth generation had been in the position of overseeing themselves. While this process had served the company well in the past, the characteristics and dynamics of the rising generation of owners suggested that a new governance model might serve the owners better.

The committee took its responsibility very seriously. They read up on family business governance and talked with other family businesses that had made the transition to an independent board. They used this input to set goals for the family governance model and to develop recommendations, which were captured in a thorough, written report. The report addressed family governance (family council, committees, leadership) as well as the board of directors. Recommendations for the board included the addition of independent directors and transitioning the role of management on the board.

The family approved the recommendations of the committee and began a search process, engaging a consultant to work with them to clarify the profile of independent directors, develop the board prospectus, and identify board candidates.

While, at the ownership level, the work to research and gain consensus on the move to an independent board took almost two years, the process for identifying and selecting directors was more rapid. The consultant's work to develop the prospectus with the governance committee and senior management was completed in two months. The requirements for directors included a combination of industry and family business experience.

Because of the numerous industry challenges media companies faced, the role of the board in evaluating strategic options for the future was crucial. At the same time, experience in the media industry was not necessarily viewed as valuable since few media companies had successfully addressed these challenges. Instead, the owners and management determined that experience with innovation and rapidly changing industry environments—particularly related to technology—would be valuable. Also valued was experience in transitioning a family business from a generation of involved owners/managers to a business where not all owners were active in management.

Within another two months, the consultant had identified a pool of candidates meeting the desired profile and had conducted phone interviews to screen them. Because the owners wanted to consider a national pool of candidates, interviews were conducted over the phone. Four months after the process was launched, the consultant recommended a short list of the most qualified candidates to the committee. The committee further narrowed the list to a handful of top candidates and scheduled face-to-face meetings with them in the following month. The candidates met with management and the committee at company headquarters. Ultimately, two independent directors were selected to add to the board.

"We recognized that the old board had gaps. We knew we were looking for certain skills," says James Schurz, chair of the Committee on Family Governance. "As a result, we made sure to talk with other family businesses who were also dealing with generational transitions."

As for surprises that occurred during the search process, Schurz acknowledges there were a few cases of "hurt and misunderstood feelings." But, he adds: "No one in my generation felt entitled to serve on the board because of their last name."

To summarize, identifying and selecting directors for an active independent board can be both stimulating and challenging, and the process may take several months to complete. While everyone fears rejection, the odds are surprisingly high that worthy candidates will accept an offer of a directorship. Also, the chances of making a bad choice are quite low, with only about 1 percent of outside directors replaced each year.

Candor and thoroughness throughout the selection process can greatly improve the chances of success. With owners who are clear on the value and role of a board, on defined responsibilities and steps in the selection process, and a thorough vetting of candidates, a good outcome is certain.

Managing the Board

When the owners of McKee Foods decided to incorporate independent directors into their company board, they knew they were going to get insightful, perceptive feedback and guidance.

What they did not expect was that the mechanics of their board were about to change as well—and for the better.

"The board meeting agendas were changed almost instantly—we went from very informal meetings to more comprehensive meetings," says Mike McKee, CEO and third-generation owner. "That, and they certainly raised the bar for me in terms of meeting preparation and the quality of information."

Many business owners are surprised to learn that the chair has significant latitude under the law to focus board attention on matters of greatest concern.

Board Insight

Above all, the chair should structure board meetings to ensure efficiency and clarity of purpose. That means managing all aspects of the board's operation, from the agenda to the meeting schedule, with an eye on the highest and best use of the directors' skill sets and time commitment.

Selecting the right board members does not ensure the board will be fully effective. It is also critical to create the appropriate atmosphere, prepare the board, and run meetings well. This chapter will help demonstrate the ways that the investment in independent directors can be leveraged for maximum impact. It will offer suggestions designed to help directors do their jobs in an atmosphere of trust and confidence. It will provide information on board organization, including forming and managing committees. And it will offer practical advice on orienting new board members, running meetings, keeping in touch with directors between meetings, and evaluating the board.

Who Manages the Board?

Managing the boardroom is a critical piece of getting the most from your board. Responsibility for top-notch performance rests primarily with the chair. So, it is important to have the best person for the job. There are two different models for board leadership—a combined chair/CEO or two separate offices.

There are pros and cons to each approach. The CEO who also fills the chair slot must be prepared to play the facilitator role, rather than being an active participant in a discussion. That means giving up control of the flow of ideas and, instead, listening to what others say and asking questions. It also means managing respected peers rather than subordinates.

The responsibilities of the chair are difficult for some CEOs, although certain types of prior experience can help. A background that includes working with others in a large group setting—where ideas and feedback are readily shared—can be very useful. Membership in peer groups such as YPO or Vistage is valuable as well.

Certain personal qualities are also valuable in a board chair. It helps to be open to change and to have an appreciation of strong management as an art form. If CEOs understand that a company is always in transition in one way or another, they believe that every idea is worthy of consideration.

With that said, many family businesses find the CEO is not the appropriate choice to serve as chair for a variety of reasons. In some cases, the chairman position is reserved for the former CEO when a next-generation family CEO is named. In businesses with a nonfamily CEO, owners are often more comfortable with a family representative as chairman. Our survey results show for businesses with a nonfamily CEO and a functioning board, 96 percent have a split chair and CEO, suggesting the nonfamily CEO is partnered with a family representative as board chair. This figure contrasts sharply with companies who have a family CEO, in which the split chair and CEO structure is in place only 56 percent of the time.

Beyond considerations of the family's role in oversight of the business, it is important to consider who can best play the critical role of managing boardroom dynamics. In situations when there is no family member ideally suited to fill the chair role, family businesses may turn to an independent director to serve as chair.

If the chair and CEO roles are split between two individuals, it is important to coordinate their responsibilities in preparing for board meetings. Because CEOs are in the business day-to-day, they may have a better sense of what to include in the agenda and what materials to provide directors in advance. The chair will need to coordinate with the CEO in preparing for meetings, and may take a back seat on preparations, instead focusing on facilitation during the meeting and managing other oversight functions.

The chair's role may include interfacing with shareholders, evaluating the board to ensure it is effective, overseeing assignment of tasks to committees, and counseling the CEO. (See appendix 7 for a sample chair job description.) Even in situations where the chair and CEO positions are filled by the same person, it is valuable to outline the role of the chair to ensure it is being fulfilled. When the CEO is filling the chair's role as well, responsibilities of the chair are often overlooked due to lack of time or experience.

Corporate bylaws usually specify that the board elect its chair every year. When first constituting a board, the board development task force (our name for the group tasked with creating the board, typically consisting of owners and perhaps a consultant and some nonfamily management) will typically decide if it wants the CEO to be the chair or if someone else would be more appropriate. If an independent chair is preferred, the task force will have to give additional consideration to the skills and experience required as well as to the time commitment expected of this individual. It is usually appropriate to pay an independent chair more than other directors to compensate for the additional time and responsibility required. As a nonexecutive chair the fees are commonly 150 to 200 percent of the other independent directors.

Advance Planning

A standard rule of thumb is that the chair (in conjunction with the CEO, if the role is split) spend about one hour of preparation time for every hour spent in session with the board. The chair should take time to reflect on each item, deliberating on ways directors can be of most help to the company.

The chair should also allow time to prepare a succinct quarterly letter to directors, updating them on important developments. The chair who is not involved intimately with the business may delegate this responsibility to the CEO. The chair also needs to allow time to plan and review other advance meeting materials, including the chief financial officer's quarterly letter, if there is one. If topics are to be presented to the board by individual managers, the chair should also prepare those people and review their presentation plans.

Where Should Meetings Be Held?

While many chairs have the tendency to schedule meetings at corporate headquarters, noncompany locations have some big advantages.

Holding board meetings "off campus" reduces the chances that the meeting will be interrupted. It also affords privacy and security, eliminating the possibility that employees will overhear (and perhaps misunderstand) the board's deliberations. Another option is to hold one meeting a year at a remote company facility, providing directors with exposure to staff and operations at another location without forcing them to make a special trip. Companies headquartered in remote locations may schedule one meeting a year at a convenient location near a major airport to reduce directors' travel time.

Whatever the specific location, the general rule of thumb is a location best suited for holding a good meeting is comfortable, easily accessible, private, and quiet.

Schedules and Topics

Meetings should be scheduled well in advance, with the next calendar year's sessions set at latest by October of the previous year. Another popular method is to take time at each meeting to schedule the meeting planned for 12 or even 24 months ahead. This ensures a running schedule of regular meetings that is always planned at least a year in advance.

Many boards also find it helpful to do some agenda planning on a year-round basis. This allows efficient management of some of the board's formal duties and responsibilities, and also provides a map for company strategic planning and implementation review.

One company, for instance, included as part of its yearly board meeting schedule a summary of plans for disposing of several board topics. At the June meeting, the chair scheduled a review of regular board responsibilities, including insurance coverage, pension plan performance, election of the general counsel, progress on a succession plan, and other topics. Review of the following year's operating and capital budgets and officer compensation was set for the November meeting. The annual audit was assigned to the March agenda.

EXHIBIT 8.1: **Sample of Yearly Board Meeting Topics**

Quarter	Date	Topics
1	3/8	Audit committee (total board) with accounting firm
2	6/4	Review of regular board responsibilities
3	8/26	Strategic plan review
4	11/28	Review of operating and capital budgets, dividends and officer compensation, organization chart and succession plan

This schedule served two purposes. First, it allowed efficient handling of most of the board's legal duties in a single meeting, which was carefully planned to cover routine topics quickly. Second, it left completely free a midyear meeting, in August, for one of the most important and potentially creative functions of the board: a review of the strategic plan. In exhibit 8.1 we show a sample board schedule. In addition to the topics in the sample schedule, updates for various business areas may be planned in advance, either by functional area (e.g., marketing, operations) or by company division, if the business has subsidiaries or geographic divisions.

Many chairs also find it helpful to set aside time during at least one meeting a year to allow directors to ask nagging questions or to suggest topics and issues the board should address in the future. As discussed later in this chapter, the chair can use the same technique to gather directors' opinions on how well the board itself is functioning. Some boards set aside the last 15–30 minutes of each board meeting for these purposes.

Preparing the Agenda

The quality of the agenda has a great impact on the quality of board deliberations. When properly prepared, the agenda can not only be an organizational tool to keep discussions on track and on schedule but an advance-planning device to help directors come to meetings well prepared. A helpful rule of thumb to keep in mind in preparing the agenda is the "80–20 rule": the tendency among most groups to spend 80 percent of their meeting time on the first 20 percent of the agenda.

Many chairs make the mistake of putting reports and background sessions at the top of the agenda. This can allow board discussion to bog down in reviewing the latest quarter's performance or the soaring advertising bill, leaving inadequate time for the critical issues at the end of the agenda. Another mistake is to organize items in a way that forces directors to sit back and listen for prolonged periods of time.

A better approach is to start the meeting with the most important issues. Then, at the end of the meeting, the chair can schedule a half-hour, or whatever time is left, to field questions on recent performance and other more routine matters. As much of this routine information as possible should be distributed to directors in writing *before* the meeting. Often, this data can be handled succinctly in the quarterly letter from the chair, CEO, or chief financial officer, as explained above. In our experience, reporting on past performance can be limited to less than 25 percent of the total meeting time, leaving about three hours at each meeting for an in-depth discussion of one or two most important issues.

Many chairs also find it helpful to make the third or fourth item on the agenda an optional or slack topic. This affords the flexibility to skip it during the meeting if the earlier, more important items take more time than planned.

Exhibits 8.2 and 8.3 offer examples of imaginary good and bad agendas. In exhibit 8.2, "Underutilized Board" presents a sleepy late-afternoon session loaded with routine reports and vague generalities. In exhibit 8.3, "Fully Leveraged Board" has put together a very specific document that weighs agenda items according to their importance and offers directors a lot of help in planning for the session.

As the Fully Leveraged Board example also shows, a good agenda includes several kinds of very specific information to help guide board discussions. First, a specific amount of time should be shown on the agenda for each topic, to let directors

---

EXHIBIT 8.2:   **Underutilized Board Agenda**
Board of Directors Meeting
May 24, 3–6 p.m.
Agenda

1. Call to Order
2. Approval of Minutes; Board of Directors Meeting Feb. 28
3. President's Report—Jim Carrier
   a. The acquisition effect on our first quarter
   b. Personnel review—salaried and hourly
   c. Profit sharing—planning update
   d. Board dates—July and October
4. Planning Report—Dick Almers
   a. Results of first quarter versus goals
   b. Update on current planning efforts
5. Sales and Marketing Report—Peter LeBrun
   a. Recap of first quarter activity
   b. Review of current situation
6. Financial Report—Larry Carrington
   a. First quarter financial results
   b. First quarter cash flow analysis
   c. Long-range cash flow forecast
7. Annual Engineering Report—Carol Lee
   a. Update on equipment
   b. Governmental affairs—environmental
   c. Future planning
8. Adjourn to Dinner

---

know in advance whether a topic is to be addressed in depth. This technique has the added advantage of allowing all board members to watch the clock and share the responsibility of keeping the meeting on schedule.

Second, the agenda requests specific responses of directors when appropriate. Sometimes, a chair might only want directors' first impressions of a key manager after they make a board presentation to help in evaluating that employee's potential. Other times, the chair may want a firm decision by the board on whether or how to proceed. Alternatively,

EXHIBIT 8.3:   **Fully Leveraged Board Agenda**

Fully Leveraged Board Board of Directors Meeting
May 24, 8 a.m.–12:45 p.m.
Agenda

8 a.m. I. Introduction of Management Team—continuing
A. Presentation by Bill, manager of Belgium plant—Please review his biography.
B. Questions of Bill from board
C. First impressions—reaction to Bill's presentation (Bill excused)

8:45 a.m. II. Owners' Brief Informational Update on Items of Interest
A. Ongoing activities
B. Operations performance
C. Financial performance

9:15 a.m. III. Status Report on expansion into Phoenix and Southwest market—some preparation materials forthcoming.

10 a.m. Break

10:15 a.m. IV. Lengthy Open Discussion of Joint Venture Opportunity—some preparation materials forthcoming.
A. Brief Update
B. Board members' share experiences and opinions
  a. How do we think about form of shared business relationships?
  b. What personal financial risks and guarantees should we be willing to take?
  c. How do we live with outside business partners in shared enterprises?

11:45 a.m. V. Review of Quarterly Information Packet Format—any suggestions

12 p.m. VI. Schedule for Future Meetings—please bring calendar

12:15 p.m. VII. Executive session

12:45 p.m. VIII. Adjourn to lunch with Charles Carroll, executive vice-president and third-generation shareholders the chair may be asking for new ideas, for help in deciding among existing choices, or simply for a chance to inform the board. Making the goal clear on the agenda as a subpoint under the item listing can be very helpful to directors who need and appreciate this kind of leadership from the chairman.

The agenda should also give information about the type of discussions directors should expect. Will the chair be promoting "a lengthy open discussion" of the topic, or just "a brief informational update" with few questions expected from the board?

Major, open-ended topics should include some leading questions as subpoints, to help guide directors' thinking before the meeting. These questions can also help directors seek out other sources of information before the meeting, if they choose.

The agenda may include stage directions on when visitors to the board session will be present and excused. After a presentation by a manager, for instance, the agenda may note that the manager will be excused following a question-and-answer session. Again, this helps directors ask the right questions at the appropriate time.

Finally, the agenda may offer information on whether additional background materials will be made available at the meeting, or whether directors should bring any personal resources with them, such as their calendars for the coming year.

As the Fully Leveraged Board agenda shows, the meeting should conclude with an executive session lasting roughly 30 minutes. This is the time when all nonboard members are excused from the room to allow the board to address any comments or concerns with complete candor. Some companies may not need the session at every meeting. However, scheduling the session every meeting allows for an opportunity to address any sensitive topics without raising questions as to why people have been dismissed. For many firms, the board will also elect to excuse the CEO and other management directors for some part of the executive sessions, if there are issues that nonmanagement directors may wish to discuss alone.

Who Should Be Invited?

As a rule, only directors should expect to attend every meeting of the board, as well as any permanent secretary to the board.

Many family companies invite some nondirectors to attend meetings, including outside advisors, such as lawyers or accountants, and members of the senior management team, the CFO and, from time to time, the COO and sales and marketing executives. In founder-led family businesses, it is often helpful to invite the founder's spouse to some meetings. He or she may benefit greatly in case of a future crisis.

The attendance of outside advisors should be kept to a minimum to ensure the candor of the boardroom. Moreover, in most cases, the chair should not permit any nondirectors to assume they will attend all board meetings. This preserves the chair's latitude to take up highly sensitive or confidential matters with only directors present—a pivotal opportunity afforded by the independent board, and one that should be maintained however possible.

One special case is when next-generation owners are invited to a meeting to provide them with exposure to the board. Involving the next generation requires carefully developed guidelines which address issues such as appropriate professional behavior and confidentiality. Additionally, it is a good idea to establish a minimum age to attend meetings, such as 25 or 30. There are a number of ways the next generation may be incorporated, including setting aside one meeting a year where all attend, or creating a schedule whereby one or two next-generation owners may attend each meeting on a rotating basis.

Whatever option is selected, it is important to stress the confidentiality of board meetings. All visitors must understand that what is said in the boardroom stays there. To that effect, some boards have attendees sign confidentiality agreements, including family members.

Helping Directors Prepare: The Board Background Book

Directors depend on the chair to get the information they need to do their job well. One effective way to accomplish that is with a board background book.

The board background book is a comprehensive, professionally presented summary of important information about the business. While compiling the book can take some time, the investment of care and effort is usually greatly appreciated by the directors and often of value to the company's executive leadership. In many ways, it reflects the owners' eagerness to help the board get off to a running start and fulfill its promise.

The board background book is best gathered in a three-ring binder with a table of contents, or on a protected website. (For a sample outline of the background book see exhibit 8.4.) The book should be provided to directors well before the first board meeting, to give them time to assimilate its contents.

EXHIBIT 8.4:   **Outline of Board Background Book**

1. *Mission Statement, History and Strategy*
   a. Preamble and Board prospectus
   b. Brief history of business, including trade publication profiles or recently written articles.
   c. One- or two-page explanation of strategy, how company makes money, industry structure, and some key industry trends. (Include summaries of the economics of the industry, the value-added chain, or the product life cycle.)
2. *Who's Who*
   a. Organizational chart of the company showing names, titles, ages, years with company, number of total

reports. Possibly include total number of employees and any relevant demographics.

b. Shareholdings by owner and type of shares, buy, -sell or shareholder agreement. Business valuation; any trustees and their legal roles. Brief paragraph noting what happens to the stock of key owners in their estates.

c. List of duly elected officers and their level and form of compensation.

d. Family tree of ownership group, including in-laws, divorces, ages, and employment background.

e. Contact information for key advisers, including lawyers, accountants, insurance agents, investment advisers, family trustees, bankers, and organizational consultants.

3. *Biographies*

a. Biographies of key executives in one or two paragraphs each, including current roles and responsibilities, past work and educational experience, ages and years with company, industry and professional associations.

b. Directors' vitae as requested and received from them.

4. *Competitors, Vendors and Customers*

a. List of top three to 10 competitors and a brief description of their ownership, size, ways of competing, and other details.

b. List of top three to 10 vendors, what is bought from them and roughly how much per year.

c. List of top three to 10 customers, what they buy from the company and roughly how much per year.

d. If available, a map of the United States showing where company does business, where it is concentrated, where it has locations and salespeople.

5. *Financial Information*

a. Very efficiently presented one-page, five-year profit-and-loss statement.

b. On the same page, a current year budget and/or coming year pro forma budget.

c. Simple balance sheet items, highlighting receivables, cash, inventories, fixed assets, debt, and equity.

EXHIBIT 8.4: *Continued*

---

d. A one-page summary of financial and/or relevant operating statistics such as return on investment, return on equity, real sales growth, inventory turns, gross margin, sales per salesperson, product development budget, percentage of sales from new products, and/or new programs.

e. A one-page outline of sales per product market category over several years, perhaps including development costs per category, gross margins and other relevant details.

6. *Audit and Estate Valuation*
   a. Most recent year's audit.
   b. Employee stock-ownership plan or insurance or estate valuation, especially funding formulas and redemption requirements, if available.

7. *Articles, Bylaws, Indemnification*
   a. Articles of incorporation and corporate bylaws.
   b. Copy of director indemnification and/or legal letter and/or insurance coverage.

8. *Other Information, If Relevant*
   a. Union status, including background on any votes, affiliations, etc.
   b. Corporate insurance coverage
   c. Results of any asset appraisals.
   d. Notation of litigation pending or expected; legal letters if appropriate, specifying exposures and status.
   e. Real estate or office space owned or leased, and terms and values if not clear in audit.
   f. Any employment contracts, stock options.
   g. Any dividend information.
   h. Pension fund information and trustees.
   i. Any ending covenants or contingent liabilities.
   j. Any particular corporate contributions, such as political or charitable.

9. *Board Schedule and Agenda*
   a. Outline of proposed dates for next four or five meetings.
   b. Agenda items planned for each meeting, such as audit report, capital budget, etc.

To provide a strategic overview of the business and industry, there are three models directors might find useful. The *economics of the industry* model brings the industry alive in the minds of directors by describing the nature of the business through numbers. It provides a general industry profit model or financial profile, laying out average ratios and explaining what they mean. It should include such facts as the percentage of sales typically provided by each type of product, the average term of receivables, the gross margins on sales, and so on. For instance, a wholesale wallpaper distributor might report that the cost of sample books is typically 6 percent of sales and generates 30 percent of new sales. Receivables tend to run 60 days because most sales are to mom-and-pop stores, and gross margins in the industry are typically 30 to 35 percent.

Another approach, a *value-added chain,* traces a typical transaction in the industry from beginning to end. It describes how contracts are made, how time is spent, and how employees are utilized, all in terms of average success rates or sales. For instance, the CEO of an industrial supplier of water-purification equipment might explain that a salesperson typically spends two weeks making 20 calls to get one appointment. Every ten appointments might lead to an average sale of $50,000. Then it might take an average of two weeks and two person-hours to install equipment at each location, and an average of an additional ten hours of labor each month to maintain the equipment. These numbers might even be refined further into average conversion rates per dollar spent or person-hour worked—a $60,000-a-year salesperson might be expected to generate $500,000 in new sales.

A third approach, the *product life-cycle picture,* explains the role of new products or services in the company's overall business and describes the typical life cycle of new offerings. The CEO might report, for instance, that 30 percent of sales comes from new products in a typical year. Each product might take two years to develop at an average cost of $500,000. Its average life span might be five years, with gross margins narrowing from 33 percent to 10 percent over that period as

increasing competition emerges or price-sensitive customers delay purchases. The value of these three approaches will
depend upon the type of industry and business in which you
operate as well as the level of knowledge directors have of
your business.

The background book is a highly valuable tool for new-
director orientation. In fact, it is sometimes helpful to hold a
separate orientation session prior to the first board meeting
to review the book, which ideally should be sent in advance.
Here is a sample agenda of a board orientation session:

- 8:30–9:15 Directors get acquainted, introduce each
  other, share backgrounds
- 9:15–10:30 Overview of industry dynamics and position within industry
- 10:30–11:00 Financial overview—budget, projections
  and performance drivers
- 11:00–12:00 Strategic plan, significant challenges/
  opportunities
- 12:00–1:00 Lunch with key management, facility tour
  if not already done
- 1:00–2:00 Director questions or comments on information in the background book and wrap-up/planning
  for first official meeting

The board background book is a living document that
should be updated as information changes—in other words,
it is a reference manual for directors. In addition to the board
book, exposure to company facilities can be valuable. In some
cases, directors may visit locations as a group. For companies with retail outlets, board members are encouraged to
visit locations near their homes. It is important to remember,
however, that there needs to be balance between the desire to
expose directors to business locations and the fact that these
visits can be very time-consuming. For this reason, it can
be helpful to periodically hold board meetings at a remote
company location to provide exposure to company locations
without demanding additional time of directors.

Preparing Advance Meeting Materials

Like the agenda, the preparatory board packet can greatly influence the quality of the time directors spend together at each meeting. Directors should receive, well in advance, the agenda and any agenda topic information, the letters from the CEO and/or chief financial officer, and up-to-date financial statements. The CFO and CEO letters update directors on the company's financial performance as compared with projections, as well as on key operating ratios, market performance, and capital expenditures. Drafts of resolutions for board consideration and other material that may need board approval can also be included.

In this mailing, most chairs include minutes from the latest meeting so directors can review them and offer any corrections. Some chairs like to send the minutes soon after the previous meeting, however, while directors' recollections are still fresh. Many do both.

Ideally, the packet should arrive before the weekend preceding the meeting; that gives directors time over one weekend to review it. It also allows time for directors to gather information on major agenda topics, if they so choose. Many family businesses find great value in sharing the background book and the agenda preparations with all the family owners.

Organizing the New Board

This section offers guidance on some basic organizational questions that may arise before the first meeting or during the board's early months.

The Importance of a Quorum

The absence of a quorum—the minimum number of members required to transact business—seldom becomes a problem for a privately held family business. Usually, the number required for a quorum is set by corporate bylaws. It is typically one more than half of the directors, or a simple majority. A quorum must be present for the board to hold a vote on anything requiring board approval.

Ideally, the chair should arrange meetings so that everyone can attend. It is also easier if the board calendar is published at least a full year in advance. If one member simply cannot be available because of a prolonged business trip or other development, most chairs go ahead with the meeting. If more than one member of a board of four to seven directors is unavailable, the session should probably be rescheduled. On larger boards with a mix of insiders and independent directors, many CEOs simplify the scheduling process by making the presence of all independent directors the primary goal.

Another option is to have members attend by phone. In some cases, specially called meetings may be held entirely via phone. Company bylaws can be written to specify members' ability to vote via phone—or even via email.

The Role of the Board Secretary

Ideally, a trusted and capable administrative aide or executive secretary to the CEO or chair can serve as secretary to the board, taking minutes, preparing advance materials, and handling other organizational matters. In some companies, the board secretary also presents routine matters to the board for action.

This person can handle other record-keeping duties as well. This should include mailing advance meeting materials and maintaining a meeting file with a record of advance materials sent to directors, including the preliminary agenda, a meeting notice, lodging arrangements, and other specifics. The board secretary should also keep track of which directors might have conflicts with regard to attending upcoming meetings, and which cannot attend.

While the administrative secretary plays a valuable role, it is important to assure an executive session without the administrative secretary.

The next best person to handle minute-keeping duties is the board facilitator, if there is one. As discussed earlier, this person serves either as a consultant to the board or as a director and helps manage board operations and guide board discussions in a productive way.

In the absence of such a person, one director—preferably an inside director, such as a shareholder or manager—can be assigned the task. All the directors may also serve in turn, preparing the minutes for a year and then handing the duty on to another director. The one-year rotation allows each director to get used to the job. The general counsel, if present at all meetings, also can keep the minutes. The general counsel typically maintains the official board minute book.

The worst choice for these tasks is the CEO, who should remain free during each meeting to focus on the discussion.

During the meeting, the person charged with preparing the minutes should note the following:

- The time, place, and date the meeting was called to order by the chairman and the names of all directors and other persons who were present
- The motion to approve the previous meeting's minutes and, if appropriate, a motion to waive reading of the minutes
- Acknowledgement of a quorum
- The times at which various people entered and left the room during the meeting
- The names of people who made reports and a brief summary of the reports
- Actions taken and the outcome of votes, including who voted for and against a measure and who abstained (on important issues, the reasons for dissents and abstentions should be recorded)
- Any conflicts of interest acknowledged by directors, and any abstention from discussions and votes involving any conflicts of interest
- Agreements or consensus reached during the meeting, as well as other items received or discussed

- The amount of time spent on very important issues, as well as a summary of important advice offered by professional advisers and any evidence of advance preparation by board members
- The motion to adjourn and the time of adjournment

Keeping the Minutes

Federal and state laws do not set forth any particular requirements for board minutes. As a result, companies' minutes vary widely in form and style. Some take only a skeletal record, primarily documenting board decisions and director votes. A motivating factor here is often the fear of legal action, because official board minutes can be used as evidence in cases involving board actions. Some owners simply want to preserve secrecy and resist any more disclosure of information about the company than is legally required.

Increasingly, though, many companies prefer to create a more complete "living record" of board deliberations, including insights and unanswered questions that arose during the meeting, and the pros and cons that were considered. While these boards are aware of the worries cited above, they reason that thorough minutes of most board sessions are likely to do more to ease suspicions than inflame them. Many find a follow-up checklist of action items raised at the board meeting to be a valuable addition to the board minutes.

Drafts of the minutes should be reviewed by the corporate counsel and the chair and presented to directors at the next meeting for corrections. Board minutes should be kept on record permanently.

Official Resolutions

An official resolution is a written statement that the board votes to approve. The law does not set forth guidelines for using formal resolutions. However, most boards consider them appropriate in at least the following instances:

- Election of officers
- Establishment of board committees and their responsibilities
- Dividend declarations
- Any amendment to the corporate charter or bylaws
- Any matter that requires formal resolution according to the law, charter, or bylaws

Forming and Managing Committees

Most boards in small to medium-sized private companies do not find it necessary to organize committees. However, for larger boards, or boards of large companies with several divisions, or those planning to go public, committees can be useful. The most common are audit, compensation, and nominating committees. Our research on committees shows that 34 percent of the respondents with active boards have committees. The average is two, although some have as many as four. Most committees in smaller firms can do their work in one meeting a year, perhaps holding a meeting for an additional hour before a regularly scheduled board session. The committees then communicate with the full board both orally and through written minutes.

The role and authority of various board committees differ from company to company, and the law does not set specific committee requirements. However, most states limit committees' authority by prohibiting them from undertaking such actions as amending the bylaws, declaring dividends, authorizing the issues of stock, or adopting an agreement of merger or consolidation.

Here is a summary of the usual roles of a few of the most common kinds of board committees. For more detailed information, refer to sample committee charters in appendix 2.

The *audit committee* should be composed of mostly independent outside directors, not management. Its job is to recommend and review selection of the company's outside auditors and to review the auditor's report. This group should also review with the independent auditors the adequacy of internal controls as well as any major changes in the company's accounting practices. When companies have an internal audit function, it reports to the audit committee.

The *nominating committee's* job is to recommend candidates to fill vacancies on the board and usually to identify desirable criteria for board membership. It may also be asked to take a special interest in succession issues, such as recommending a successor to the CEO or other senior managers. Some nominating committees set emergency succession procedures in the event the CEO should become unable to serve. In larger companies, the nominating committee may expand its role to include overall governance. Often named a governance committee, additional responsibilities include setting committee structure and committee membership and evaluating board performance.

The *compensation committee* is usually charged with ensuring that compensation is competitive and appropriate to the company's strategic and human resources objectives. Management directors should be excluded from the compensation committee, since it periodically reviews the annual salary, bonus, and other benefits for the CEO and other senior managers. Sometimes the compensation committee oversees all the company's key human-resource policies.

While some companies authorize an executive committee, a subset of the board that is empowered to make decisions on behalf of the full board, this approach is not recommended. It is important to engage the full board in all the board's important work. Board telephone calls can readily resolve any item requiring board attention before the next meeting.

Although committees are very useful, committees should not take on tasks that are the responsibility of the full board, such as strategic planning. To counter this, committees should focus mostly on preparation work for full board discussion and approval to ensure that the full board is involved in key issues.

For the committee structure to be effective, the full board must have confidence in the preliminary work of committees and any recommendations forwarded by committees. Failing that, the overall board may waste time by addressing issues in committee and then revisiting them as a full board. With that in mind, when recruiting board members, think about skills needed for particular committees so that the full board will trust the recommendations of committee members.

Running the First Meeting

The first meeting of a newly constituted board can be both an exhilarating and a nerve-wracking experience for the chair and the management team. For many, it poses new challenges in self-expression and interpersonal relationships.

Several special measures can help ensure a good start for the board. First, it is helpful to schedule a brief social session of a half hour or so before the meeting, to allow directors to meet and talk informally over coffee. This session should be noted on the agenda, so that directors know the exact start time of the official meeting and recognize that social time was scheduled at the start. It is important to signal from the first meeting that the chair respects directors' time and will stick to the agenda. Another option is a separate orientation session prior to the first meeting, as discussed earlier. If directors have already had an opportunity to meet each other in an orientation or dinner prior to the meeting, a social session at the beginning of the meeting is not necessary.

If the board has not held a formal orientation session covering this information, the first agenda item should usually be a brief recap by the chair and/or owners represented on the board of the rationale for setting up the board. The chair should also introduce each director briefly, going beyond the biographical data in the board background book to explain the special value each person brings to the table. The chair at this point should also express his or her pleasure at having each director on the board, conveying personal appreciation for each person's unique potential contribution. At that point, the chair might ask directors to say a little about their background, why they agreed to serve on the board, and what they hope to gain from the experience. (Additionally, any time new directors join the board, they should be introduced and given an opportunity to share something about themselves.)

This meeting also affords a valuable opportunity to glean first impressions from knowledgeable outsiders. Some chairs find they can learn a lot from their directors' reactions to the board background book.

The chair should not hesitate to consider a variety of get-acquainted techniques at this meeting. A videotaped plant visit with employee interviews, a multi-department presentation of the life cycle of a product, or a drive around company locations in an executive van might be enjoyable and helpful for directors. The goal should be to convey, as efficiently as possible, a flavor of the business. Again, if this information has already been covered in a separate orientation, the chair can follow a more traditional board meeting agenda at the first meeting.

While an orientation session will cover company background, it may still be useful at the first meeting to create opportunities for directors to interact and get to know each other better. One idea is to introduce a topic that is likely to get everyone involved. For instance, the chair might ask each director to talk about how he or she sees the world and the economy changing over the next two or three years as it relates to his or her own business. This usually leads to a discussion of key issues, and it can uncover some common ground and begin building affinity among board members.

Between-Meeting Communications

The information packet sent before each regular board meeting is usually the major communication between directors and the company between board meetings.

Ideally, directors should receive other relevant information from the company between meetings, although this is not always possible. Some companies provide board members with any information in the press on themselves, their industry or their competitors. Others may provide updates of consulting or financial industry analysts' reports on their industry. Directors should be included on the mailing list for employee or customer newsletters as well. Many directors also appreciate a subscription to the industry trade magazine and, if relevant, a copy of the company catalog, major advertisements, or promotional material.

A simple note of gratitude after a particularly successful board meeting is greatly appreciated by directors. The point of staying in touch is not only to keep directors informed but to stimulate thinking about the business, alerting them to prospects and ideas that might be relevant.

The CEO or the chair should always feel free occasionally to consult directors between meetings for advice and counsel, to update them on important issues, or to invite the director to a private lunch. Directors should not, however, be invited as advisers to internal management meetings. While board members might sit in on occasional meetings to observe or contribute to a brainstorming session, they should not be made to feel like a part of management, or expected to deliver professional services free of charge.

Usually, major developments can be covered in the chair or CEO's quarterly letter to directors. If the chair and CEO position are held by separate individuals, both officers may send an update letter to other directors prior to the board meeting. But anything special or unusual might prompt a call or note to directors. Three straight months of record sales or the successful recruitment of a top-flight manager might be examples. By the same token, anything that damages the long-term health of the company—such as a significant worsening of labor-management tensions or the loss of a major lawsuit—should be communicated to the board.

Evaluating and Changing the Board

The quality of the board's performance and contributions should be a continuing concern for the chair.

Ideally, when the board is constituted the chair should set up an evaluation process. In some cases, the ownership group may identify the desire for an annual board-evaluation process when they articulate the need for an independent board. Unfortunately, our survey shows only 18 percent of boards have an evaluation process. However, that number increases to 42 percent for those boards with two or more independent directors.

There are different ways to handle board evaluations. The preferred option is a written survey that each board member completes on his or her own and turns in to the chair or an agreed upon third party to tabulate the results. The evaluation focuses on various areas of board structure, process, and culture. See exhibit 8.5 for examples of evaluation questions. (A more comprehensive board evaluation form is provided in appendix 6.) In rare instances, firms also conduct a peer evaluation of each individual director. This process requires great maturity and preparation of the board. To start, individual directors can evaluate what they feel they are contributing to the board along with a self-assessment of areas where they could contribute more. Directors may also evaluate their fellow directors on the same criteria as they evaluate themselves. This can be done with the chair or a consultant. Peer-director review should first focus on developmental improvement. If the evaluation process is available to the family owners, or for grading contribution, it is recommended that it be done by a skillful chair or with a consultant.

It is the chair's responsibility to administer the evaluation process, although the chair may rely on an outside consultant or the governance committee to help structure and tabulate results. Results should be presented to the full board as a general summary. Peer-evaluation results are only shared with respect to general trends across the full board, not singling out the performance of an individual director.

The chair should meet with directors individually to talk about their performance and how they are feeling about the board. It is often helpful to hold these informal, individual sessions with each director at least once every two years. This

EXHIBIT 8.5:   **Sample Evaluation Questions**

- Are the role and responsibilities of the board clearly defined and understood?
- Does the board stay informed about trends and issues critical to the company's future performance?
- Does the board dedicate adequate time to identifying, analyzing, and discussing strategic issues?
- Does the board receive the appropriate information to fulfill its governance responsibilities?
- Have the shareholders' objectives and expectations been adequately communicated to the board?

permits the board member to offer suggestions privately, as well as to offer any hints that the group or its individual members are not performing as well as they should.

Many chairs once a year open up an hour to an hour-and-a-half on the board agenda to discuss the quality of the board experience. While this group discussion will be less free than private conversations, it can offer valuable insight into the general direction of the board. This session may serve as a more informal alternative to a written survey.

Some chairs or ownership groups employ consultants, either on a sustained or one-time basis, to help evaluate and strengthen their boards. This can be particularly helpful if the board seems stagnant or troubled. An industrial psychologist, organizational-development expert, or some other management specialist has the advantage of being able to interview directors confidentially to glean a sense of how the board's functioning might be improved.

If a director needs to be relieved of his position, the chair should take responsibility for the decision, rather than falling back on concerns raised by peers or a consultant as an excuse. While removing a director can be an uncomfortable process, it is always best to approach the director in a straightforward, appreciative, and empathic fashion.

In conclusion, careful planning with emphasis on the most important issues facing the company is crucial to the success of the board. The board agenda, advance meeting materials, meeting schedule, and other board communications should all be designed to guide the board toward its highest and best use, ensuring the continuity and strategic success of the company.

Few organizational requirements are set forth in the law for boards of directors, leaving the chair considerable latitude in guiding board discussion toward matters of the greatest concern to the company and its owners. The chair should structure the board, from the minute-taking process to committee structure, in a way that will ensure efficiency and clarity of purpose and reflect the values of the company's owners.

The chair can take several steps to help directors do their jobs effectively, from providing needed information to encouraging positive and trusting relationships with key people in the company. Using the special talents of board members to the fullest is one of the best investments of time the chair can make.

Making the Most of Your Board

For many family firms, working with an independent board is a new experience that poses unforeseen rewards—and challenges. Every board meeting can be an adventure, an exploration of the unknown. The spontaneous interaction of experienced business owners, entrepreneurs, and managers facing common questions can spark insights and ideas gratifying to all involved. The result may be breakthrough thinking—a contribution that strips away burdensome preconceptions and often transcends the capability of any individual board members.

"I've never seen a group of people get off to such a running start in my life!" says one chair of his independent board. To his surprise, directors engaged each other in a lively debate at their very first meeting. "There's synergy there, no doubt about it."

Yet, managing this kind of peer interaction does not come easily to many board chairs. For the business leader accustomed to being in charge and largely unaccountable, a boardroom where directors ask tough questions and make suggestions that push management out of its comfort zone can be strange and threatening turf.

This chapter takes a close look at how the chair can help a board function at its greatest potential. It offers insight into the new psychological and emotional challenges the chair (and management team) may confront with the board. It provides suggestions for sparking productive and creative boardroom discussions. And it describes some early-warning signs that can help the chairman realize the board may be underused or struggling.

Managing the Boardroom

One of the responsibilities of the chair is to ensure that the strengths of each director are leveraged in the boardroom. When preparing for board meetings, chairs should be mindful of directors' personal strengths, personalities, and preferences. The following suggestions show how this can be useful in reaping the full benefits of the board and in averting unproductive conflict:

Tap Individual Directors' Strengths and Experience

While general board discussion can be a powerful tool, some individual directors have far more to offer on certain topics than do others. Some chairs ask directors with specialized knowledge to prepare in advance to address the board on certain topics. Others find it helpful to write down, for their own reference, follow-up questions on important agenda items, marked with the initials of the person best suited to address them.

Avoid Setting Up Conflicts

While healthy disagreement among directors can be productive, it is best to avert deep divisions on the board. If a chair senses a potential dispute, he might discuss the issue with directors before the board meeting. Asking ahead of time the views of those who are potentially opposed can calm tensions and enables the chair to weigh various courses of action.

Manage the Conversation So No One Dominates

A single director can cast a pall on an entire board by monopolizing the discussion. This poses a challenge to the chair, who must curb that person's verbosity without squelching a healthy interchange. Many chairs find it helpful in such cases to introduce discussions by saying, "Let's go around the table, and I'd like each of you to offer your thoughts."

Consider Allowing Another Director to
Facilitate a Board Session

The board may find that change in facilitation style under a different leader may unlock fresh thinking. This technique is particularly effective when the chair or CEO has strong opinions he or she may wish to defend. When guided by someone with a different facilitation style, this change in assignment may also free up fresh thinking in the board.

Facilitating Breakthrough Thinking

The effective independent board draws on a unique and powerful resource: a shared eagerness among members to tackle tough problems. Often directors working together can achieve creative or innovative solutions to problems that no individual member would have generated alone, proving the maxim that the whole is greater than the sum of the parts. Many CEOs, of course, strive constantly to achieve such creativity in management. What is so special about breakthrough thinking at the board level?

Consider this example: One CEO, discouraged by an industry shakeup and the untimely departure of his son from the business, decided that his 20-year struggle to grow the company just was not worth it anymore. He told his independent board that he wanted to sell out, and his directors began helping him shore up management and organize financial data.

But the more the CEO shared his heaviness of spirit with directors, the more he recovered his own excitement and commitment. Ultimately, with the directors' encouragement, he decided to keep the company and share more of its equity with top management and an employee stock-ownership plan. "What I'm doing here really has value, and it ought to work," he told his board. "And no one out there is going to appreciate it as much as we do!"

Another board was so impressed with a CEO's board-room profit analysis that members persuaded him to make the same presentation to employees. To do that, the reluctant CEO had to overcome a decades-old tradition of secrecy at his family-held firm. But the result was a new excitement among workers about the company's future— and a lasting commitment by the CEO to a new openness in management.

Breakthroughs like this are priceless—and often unattainable for even the most capable CEOs alone, no matter how long they agonize over the problem. How does one create the kind of boardroom climate that encourages breakthrough thinking? The challenge to the chair is to unleash the collective power of the directors' thinking. This can require a certain self-discipline that is new to many business leaders.

"The chair makes the board what she wants," says a director of one private company. The management team "throws everything out on the table, and we really work at it. As a result, we have come up with ideas as a group that none of us would have individually."

That kind of candor, many experienced directors agree, is a powerful catalyst to effective board performance. Let us take a closer look at this and other attitudes shared by many effective board members. While the board chair facilitates the meeting, the CEO and his senior management team are the ones who are opening themselves up to independent directors' suggestions and scrutiny. So, comments in this section are focused on the CEO and his receptivity to directors' counsel.

The Importance of Being Open

Making the most of the board demands a degree of openness unfamiliar to many CEOs. It often requires bending management traditions dictating that "you just don't divulge" information about matters of concern, one owner says.

"If the CEO really thinks about it and takes an inventory of what he's worried about, those are the things he has to talk to the board about," shares Clayton Mathile, who built and sold IAMS Company, then founded Aileron, a nonprofit organization that provides educational programs and other resources to business owners. "No matter how sensitive the issue, he's got to tell the board."

A prerequisite for this kind of candor is mutual respect. "You're dealing with peers. They're as smart [as] or smarter than you are, so don't try to outwit them," Mathile says. "Just lay it on the table. Say, 'I've got this problem,' and toss it out there. Chances are, they'll gobble it up. These folks are aggressive and bright, and they're looking for challenges—and they're eager to help."

Many CEOs find it helpful to remember that learning was among their goals in naming independent directors in the first place. This may not always be comfortable. "We wanted directors who would give us feedback—and they have made me squirm!" says the CEO of a family-owned manufacturing business. "At times, it has been unpleasant. At times, I wished they would go away."

But a defensive reaction—falling back on routine, unimaginative agendas, jamming board meetings full of operating reports and rubber-stamp resolutions—can cripple the board.

"The CEO gets out of it what he puts into it," says one director. "If you don't share information, you don't allow the directors to experience, touch, and taste it, you're going to raise elements of doubt, and the board just won't work." To be an effective director, he adds, "you almost have to feel like one of the family."

Making the leap to candor with directors can yield unforeseen benefits. One CEO's three-year association with independent directors not only taught him to share financial information but also lent the self-confidence he needed to end his own long professional isolation. After a lifetime of holding high-profile, successful executives in his city at a distance, he began reaching out to others for friendships and business contacts, empowered by a new sense of self-esteem and confidence in his own abilities.

How Do I Deal With All the Questioning?

Most CEOs feel some reservations about the prospect of a rigorous, potentially critical, boardroom session. "When you have your first board meeting with these outsiders, a whole lot of embarrassing things can happen," says one CEO. "My board said, essentially, 'Why are were here?' I said I needed some help in running the business, and I named several areas. 'OK,' the board said. 'Where do you want to the business to be five years from now?' I didn't have any idea. Strategic planning was a strange term to me."

Many CEOs find it helpful to remember a few rules of thumb in dealing with board input.

Rule One: Avoid Over-explaining   The CEO should resist the understandable tendency during board sessions to become defensive—to over-explain the ways the business is different, or why a certain suggestion will not work.

Rule Two: Listen   A related demand on the CEO is to listen. The CEO does not need to embrace all board suggestions, but should consider them seriously. One CEO learned the value of this insight when the board recommended that the CEO use an industrial psychologist to help evaluate a candidate for senior management (due to some concerns they had when they interviewed the candidate). For reasons that seemed sound to the board, the industrial psychologist strongly recommended rejecting the candidate, reinforcing the value of the board's suggestion.

Rule Three: Be Patient A common source of discouragement among CEOs is their own unrealistic expectations. The CEO seeking a quick fix or panacea for complex business problems is certain to be disappointed. No board can act overnight to resolve problems that have been months or years in the making. Directors need time to familiarize themselves with a business and its culture, to mull over problems, and to wrestle with alternative solutions.

Rule Four: Remember the Board Is There to Help Despite such efforts to maintain a constructive attitude, CEOs sometimes emerge from boardroom sessions feeling a bit "beaten up." Board feedback sometimes seems inappropriate. "How do I cope with getting advice I know isn't on target?" the CEO wonders.

Despite such misgivings on the part of the business leaders, many directors like the challenge of wrestling with amorphous or unformed issues. And none expect the CEO to be perfect! Many CEOs find it helpful to remember that their directors would not have agreed to serve if they did not already respect and admire them.

Rule Five: Maintain a Sense of Humor Few qualities are more effective in creating goodwill and cooperation than a sense of humor on the part of the CEO. An ability to share a joke and laugh at oneself is universally valued, and it can be helpful in cutting tension.

Many CEOs find it helpful to remind themselves, too, of the board's true role. Its offerings are advice and counsel—a smorgasbord of ideas, suggestions, and feedback for the business leadership.

Rule Six: Remember, Most of All, Directors Do Not Want to Make Decisions They know the CEO knows more than they do and rarely do they insist on their point of view. That said, most CEOs appreciate that good questions from directors deserve ample consideration.

Creating an Appropriate Board Culture

A family business board works best when there is a spirit of mutual respect between independent directors and management. To achieve this, management needs to be open to board input. By the same token, the board needs to be open to its own biases, particularly with regard to family business dynamics. That sets up a delicate balancing act—being supportive of management yet also holding them accountable. Thinking through how a board can best fulfill these roles can be helpful in setting board culture.

The board can fulfill its promise when these two dynamics are understood and accepted. To that end, respect is enhanced when directors feel completely comfortable letting others know their personal assumptions and biases when offering advice—as well as considering the advice of other board members.

With that in mind, there are two dimensions of boardroom culture to consider: supportive versus critical, and fiduciary versus advisory (see box below). The former captures the degree to which the board generally functions to support and build upon the ideas of management versus the degree to which the directors view their role as identifying problems and finding solutions. The latter refers to the degree to which the directors see themselves as fiduciaries, with the primary responsibility of holding management accountable for delivering on results, as opposed to functioning in an advisory capacity in which they provide input for management consideration (Exhibit 9.1).

Board Insight

The ideal family business board is one that is more fiduciary than advisory—meaning the directors take seriously their responsibility for ensuring the business is well run and the needs of owners are understood. At the same time, the ideal board is also supportive of the owners and the business, rather than critical. With those features in place, the boardroom becomes a place of partnership, collaboration and shared purpose, while still protecting the rights of owners and ensuring the business is well-managed.

EXHIBIT 9.1:   **Axes of Board Style and Role**

Supportive

	Quadrant 1	Quadrant 2	
	Ideal Family Business Model (Rare)	Entrepreneurial Company Model— Early Stage	
ROLE Fiduciary			Advisory
	Quadrant 4	Quadrant 3	
	Public Company Model	Entrepreneurial Model—Late Stage (Rare)	

Critical

STYLE

While the CEO and his team have a great influence on boardroom culture by the manner in which they receive advice and counsel from the board, the chair has the most direct control over boardroom culture. In cases where the chair and CEO roles are split, it is the chair's responsibility to ensure candor and collaboration in the boardroom, to coach the CEO on receiving advice openly, and to redirect director criticism and direct comments toward a supportive tone. When the CEO fills the chairman slot as well, he must be especially careful to guard against defensiveness—graciously accepting input into his ideas and recognizing that the board has a fiduciary responsibility to the full ownership group to ensure the business is well-run.

Creativity through Leadership

For many chairs, one of the first steps toward creating a productive boardroom atmosphere is to cast off stereotypes. A formal boardroom atmosphere dominated by overly rehearsed management speeches and multimedia presentations would be stifling for most directors. A more informal atmosphere that encourages discussion and debate is much preferred. That said, directors will expect a preplanned, well-organized and professionally run meeting.

Thorough preparation by the chair can help set a rigorous tone that lasts throughout the board meeting. Both advance mailed materials and conversations with directors before the meeting can create a sense of expectancy that will spark good discussions.

"I operate a little like a football coach, trying to get the players in the right frame of mind on the key issues before they even come into the room," says one chair. "That way, everybody can hit the street running. We don't have to start out saying, 'Let me fill you in on everything that has happened since we last met.'"

The chair can set a productive tone by his or her conduct toward directors. One chair, for instance, shuns excessive formality in favor of a "let's get down to business" approach, one director says. "His attitude is, 'I respect your time.' There aren't any constraints like, 'Shall we have a motion?' then something is moved and seconded and buried. All that stuff is gone."

While leadership is crucial in the board chair, this should not be construed as a mandate to overstructure meetings. Striving to contain and control every discussion is a common pitfall for inexperienced chairs. Many topics are better suited to open-ended conversation. Allowing an hour or so on the agenda to muddle through a topic can be highly productive. This approach might be appropriate, for instance, if a CEO is stalled on how to begin thinking about choosing a successor.

"I'm concerned about this, and I know I should be concerned," the CEO might tell the board. "But I don't even know enough about it to manage the conversation. What are your thoughts on defining the succession process?" However, it is important to manage directors' expectations in this type of session so they understand the intent of the open-ended discussion. It should not be perceived that the chair is not organized or that the ideas are not being weighed seriously. Even in open ended discussions, the chair should summarize the conclusions and define next steps that will be taken.

Sparking Productive, Creative Discussions

Once the ground rules are clear, how can the board chair help spark the kind of freewheeling, candid interchange most likely to yield helpful results?

Let us take a look at some techniques many business owners have found helpful.

- *Start impartially.* Invite open, spontaneous discussion by introducing an issue impartially. "I see this as a tough decision. Here are some of the pros and cons," the chair might say. Or, "I'm torn between two alternatives."

- *Collect private information.* Ask each director to write down their views or first impressions on a topic. Then go around the table to avoid groupthink, or silence from any who may be unsure.

- *Challenge your own thinking.* "I'm having some second thoughts about our direction on this. What do you think?" is a possible opener.

- *Appoint a devil's advocate.* Some business owners take aside one director before the meeting and ask this individual to take an opposing position on a particular topic.

- *Split into smaller groups.* If the board is at loggerheads, the CEO might ask directors to break up into smaller groups, brainstorm for a while, and return to the full board with joint recommendations.

- *Do not hesitate to defer major decisions.* The CEO should not hesitate to defer a board decision on important issues to the next meeting, particularly if the question has come to an impasse.

- *Limit participation by outside advisers.* While experts' input can be valuable, most CEOs find it best to invite them one at a time.

Using Committees to Increase
Board Effectiveness

The chair plays a critical role in ensuring the board is addressing the right issues in a productive way. Committees are another tool that can be used to leverage the board's time and expertise.

Board committees are used to focus the attention and expertise of directors on some of the most crucial and routine of board tasks. Typically, committees are used by larger, more mature boards. A committee structure does not make sense unless a board has eight or more members.

In our survey we found that boards with independent directors are more likely to have a committee structure, which is not surprising. It is common to identify an independent director with a strong financial background to contribute to the audit process. And, independent directors are often involved in the compensation committee, as it can be helpful—when family members are involved in senior management—to assign the reviewing of management compensation to the independent directors.

Because issues related to evaluation and compensation of family executives can be so delicate, independent directors can have a great impact. Take the case of one second-generation family business owned by three siblings, two sisters and a brother. One sister served as CEO, and her siblings, who were not active in the business, were board members. The siblings pushed for an independent board because they had concerns about the level of their sister's compensation.

When two independent directors were added to the board, they became the compensation committee. Their first request was to hire a compensation consultant to evaluate the level of industry compensation. Once they received the consultant's report, they informed the board that the sister's compensation was not only in line, it was a bit lower than industry average.

While committees can be a useful tool to increase board productivity, they need to be managed well.

Board Insight

Before launching a committee, a committee charter should be established outlining the role and responsibilities and authorities of the committee (see appendix 2 for sample committee charters.)

One concern regarding having too many committees is that they are taking on business that should rightly come before the overall board, such as strategic or financial planning. To counter this, committees should recommend action for full board approval to ensure the full board is involved in key issues. Another challenge is delegating responsibility to committees. The overall board may waste time by addressing issues in committee and then revisiting them as a full board. Of course, often the committee's thinking can be enhanced by full-board dialogue.

It is the chair's responsibility to ensure that committees are used effectively. The chair should take responsibility for reviewing the committee agenda to confirm that the committee is sticking to its charter, ensuring there is appropriate communication between committees and the full board, and evaluating committee performance on a periodic basis.

Troubleshooting

Some early warning signs can help alert the chair to potential problems on the board. While many factors can cause a board to function poorly, they typically fall into four categories: The unimaginative agenda, the inflexible individual, the contested board, and the lack of follow-up.

The Unimaginative Agenda

Several developments can signal the need for a more imaginative, challenging agenda. If board meetings seem to drag, it is a warning sign. Members of effective boards typically report that their meeting time flies.

If meetings seem comfortable and routine, the chair probably is not posing challenging or important enough questions. As unappealing as it may seem, management should *expect* to feel uncomfortable and on edge for at least part of every meeting.

If directors begin arriving late and leaving early, it is a sign that they are bored, poorly managed, or unsuited for their jobs. The chair should quickly explore the reasons for their apparent lack of interest.

Another danger sign is the recurrence of the same agenda topics. Any sense that agenda topics are being recycled from meeting-to-meeting or year-to-year is an indication the board is performing routine functions rather than serving as a forum for advice and counsel.

As discussed, a prevalence of management reports and other operating recaps reflects a backward focus. This is a signal that management is not stretching to anticipate future issues and questions and present them to the board. In most cases, reporting can be structured so it takes less than one-fourth of total meeting time, leaving at least three hours at each meeting for critical issues.

Some chairs fall into the trap of using their boards merely as a source of information. This is a natural tendency, particularly on the part of entrepreneurs who are used to managing subordinates rather than peers. But it misses the opportunity to leverage the board's fullest potential, and it makes directors feel diminished as well.

The Inflexible Board Member

Another set of warning signals can indicate the presence of a member ill-suited for the position of director. One of the most common problems among individual directors is inflexibility. Sometimes, directors are so wedded to a set of assumptions that they perceive all issues in black and white from that rigid frame of reference. These persons are prisoners of their particular experience.

Such an attitude compromises one of the principal sources of board creativity—the ability to tap "flexible frameworks," or different viewpoints on the same problems. Even though the director's viewpoint may be partly correct, it becomes an impediment rather than a stimulus to problem solving.

A similar problem is the tendency among some directors to relate every topic to their own businesses. While sharing information from one's own business is often helpful, the director must be sensitive to the fine line between being helpful and being wedded to his personal frame of reference.

Perhaps most disappointing are instances in which individual directors simply fail to fulfill their promise. The third-generation business owner from an industry bristling with problems analogous to your own, for instance, might seem the ideal director for your third-generation family business. But, if this person lacks the depth and thoughtfulness required to be an effective director, he may hamper rather than help board discussion. Most chairs find a candid and direct solution the best recourse in these situations. Relieving ineffective directors of their duties in a straightforward but appreciative and empathic way is usually the best course of action for all concerned. "If a director has a negative attitude, and people don't like working with that person, that's unhealthy," says an experienced director. "It takes the energy out of the room. It's better if the chair simply 'disinvites' that person."

The Contested Board

Sometimes, problems spring from shareholder politics or from tensions among directors. Some directors tend to view themselves as representatives of certain constituencies, such as a shareholder group or the local community. "Well, I've talked to all the nonemployed shareholders, and I want to tell you, they all feel the same way," such a director may say. These directors may withdraw into their constituency viewpoint so frequently that they force other directors to take opposing points of view, fractionalizing the board. This poses a major problem to the board's functioning. This can be a rough problem to resolve. If a shareholder dispute is the source of the tensions, some chairs try loading the board with shareholders—a remedy that seldom works.

A more productive method is to hold a family or shareholder meeting to discuss shareholder differences. This may presage the formation of a family council, which can serve as a permanent forum for shareholder issues, a topic that will be discussed in the following chapter.

Engaging a consultant or expert in organizational behavior to conduct a group consultation also can help improve group dynamics on the board or improve the board-management relationship. An experienced adviser can help the board, management, and shareholders better understand their working relationship and use the information to improve the effectiveness of the board.

The Lack of Follow-up

In our experience, many directors' greatest frustrations are ideas or concerns raised in board meetings that are ultimately never addressed. To resolve this problem, the chair should step in to keep track of issues that are raised and, at the end of the meeting, circle back and clarify the next steps in addressing those issues. One way to follow through is to report at the next board meeting the steps that were taken to follow up on issues raised at the prior meeting. If the list of issues and next steps is captured in board minutes, it will be easier for the board to track follow-through.

Special Uses for Independent Directors

Many business leaders find unique and special ways to involve independent directors in their businesses. Here are a few examples of roles directors can usefully undertake:

- Interviewing key recruits, not only to assess the candidate but to sell the recruit on the company
- Interviewing recent hires to gather first impressions from a fresh perspective
- Attending corporate ceremonies, such as groundbreakings or "Founder's Days"
- Meeting with lenders regarding a major refinancing or other transaction
- Addressing occasional management meetings on special or timely topics
- Sitting in on important strategic-planning sessions relevant to the director's expertise
- Acting informally as mentor to a successor or next generation of management

In addition to making contributions to management in areas related to their expertise, directors with family business expertise can contribute at the family level. Examples of director involvement at this level include the following:

- Periodically attending family meetings or functions to build relationships with shareholders
- Speaking on topics where the director has unique expertise at shareholder meetings or family council meetings or at a next-generation owners meeting
- Advising shareholders on setting up a family council or holding family meetings
- Sharing examples of effective shareholder or family practices from their family business

Interaction with shareholders is most common in more mature family businesses with multiple generations of owners. In our next chapter, we will discuss the interaction between shareholders and board in older family businesses.

Holding director retreats to probe major issues and build effective relationships between directors and management is becoming more widely recognized as a way to engage directors in strategic discussions. While retreats are most common among large companies, some smaller private firms use them as well. These two-day sessions at a resort or other comfortable, private site typically include two or more formal board sessions, usually in the mornings. Afternoons are reserved for informal activities and recreation.

One company invited key professional advisers and suppliers to a morning retreat session to give a state-of-the-world address to directors and managers. In this session, the company's insurance broker, banker, accountant, industrial psychologist and others were each asked to summarize recent changes in their industry or profession and predict how those changes would affect the company.

Finally, each participant was asked to recommend ways they might be of greater service to the company, such as by providing asset reappraisals, risk analyses, and so on. At the same session, the company's management made a brief presentation on its strategic direction and developments in its industry—again, to help its advisers and suppliers prepare to serve its needs. Retreats can be expensive, but many companies that use them for well-planned business purposes believe the benefits outweigh the expense.

Every meeting with a new independent board can be an adventure, an exploration into the unknown. The dynamics of effective boards can spark breakthrough thinking—insights and ideas exciting to all involved, and which transcend the capabilities of any individual participant.

The role of the board chair is to tap a unique and powerful resource common to effective boards: a shared eagerness among members to tackle tough issues. This can require some unfamiliar skills, including an ability to let directors know what is expected of them, to permit open-ended discussions, and to encourage creativity and spontaneity among members.

At the same time, the open, rigorous interchange of the boardroom can pose a challenge, and even discomfort, to the business leaders unaccustomed to working in a forum of peers.

Effective chairs find ways to tap the best in individual directors, as well as the best in the board as a group. They remain mindful of directors' individual strengths and weaknesses and periodically offer constructive feedback to the board. They watch for trouble signs, including any failure on their own part to challenge the board, and they constantly observe the board process to ensure the board is delivering on its goal of improving the effectiveness of the business.

10

Linking Family and Business Governance in Later Generations

A common conception about family business throughout the world holds that the first generation builds
the business and later generations harvest the business rather
than reinvesting for long-term success. Nonetheless, many
family businesses strive to achieve a lasting legacy. A strong,
independent board of directors is one tool to strengthen the
business. But, the board alone cannot ensure survival. A supportive family ownership group, organized to work in support of the board and the business, is crucial as well.

As the shareholder base expands and becomes more
diverse over time, ensuring healthy shareholder relations
becomes more important and more complicated. Harnessing
the power of a cohesive, committed family shareholder base
provides great strength to a company. Conversely, managing
disparate family interests can sap management energy and
distract the CEO from pressing business issues. And while
an effective independent board can be of great help in perpetuating the family business, directors must enjoy the trust
of family shareholders and communicate well with them to
exercise needed creativity and insight.

The focus of this chapter is on the ownership groups in the
second generation or beyond, or those who aspire to reach

and surpass this milestone. Later stage family businesses typically have larger ownership groups and more sophisticated businesses. These create challenges in clarifying roles and responsibilities and in creating effective relationships between the family and the business, which requires more sophisticated governance that, in turn, can be hard work. The investment is well warranted, however, as a cohesive ownership group provides a significant competitive advantage to family enterprises. Among others, benefits include speed of decision making and a longer-term horizon on investment decisions, often described as "patient capital."

Here, we discuss the evolving needs of family businesses across generations, the importance of a family governance system to support the business governance system, and the tricky issues that are embedded in designing and managing these systems.

Stages in the Evolving Family Business

Shareholder relations in family businesses typically become more complex as the second generation of family owners grows older and their offspring (the third generation) approach the age at which they will assume an important ownership role. (This transition may happen earlier in large families with in-laws involved.) The ties binding the family can loosen or fray at this point. Often, the cohesive influence of the founder or another early business leader is waning. Further, the death of key first-generation family members may weaken the shareholders' sense of unity and common origin.

The emerging generation of shareholders may have differing expectations of the business. Cousins are usually not bonded as closely as brothers and sisters. They may demand greater financial freedom, including a liquid market for their shares. They may disagree on appropriate levels of dividends, debt, growth, and profitability for the business. Their expanding numbers may complicate the selection of future managers. They may have conflicting views on how family members should be employed and compensated in the business. In a growing business, the changing strategic needs of the company can complicate management at the same time, heightening capital requirements and sometimes demanding an entirely new style of management or even a new corporate structure.

All these conflicts and hurdles are perfectly normal and natural. Yet failure to anticipate them can waste an opportunity to harness the power of an expanding, potentially committed shareholder base. At worst, it can lead to serious shareholder disputes, liquidity and capital problems, or management crises that profoundly affect the role of the board and even force many family businesses into extinction.

How can owners and directors anticipate these hurdles and plan to surmount them effectively? Our experience and study of evolving family businesses suggest that many pass through fairly predictable stages of development. While each family business is unique, many evolve at varying rates through three basic stages of ownership. Understanding these stages and anticipating the challenges posed by transition from one to the next can help ensure a stable family legacy.

In stage one, the earliest or entrepreneurial stage, a founder or founding partners often comingle management and ownership concerns. The primary shareholder issues are relatively simple: protection for the spouse (or spouses) in the event of injury or death of the founder(s), estate planning to minimize tax liabilities for the future, and questions of leadership transition typically take top priority. Little or no formal family organization is needed at this stage. Communication tends to be simple and spontaneous.

The interests of family and business often overlap heavily at this stage, making it difficult to see where family members' business concerns end and personal ones begin. The business commands much or most of its owners' time and energy, often requiring great personal sacrifices.

In the second ownership stage, the shareholder base often takes the form of a family partnership among siblings. In this stage, maintaining teamwork and family harmony typically dominate owners' concerns. The interests of the family and business, while diverging somewhat, are often still closely entwined, and family meetings may be fairly informal, over a joint dinner or other casual get-together. Some families— depending upon the size and complexity of the business, family culture, size of the ownership group, and level of owners' involvement in the business—may move to more formal meetings at this stage.

Ownership concerns become vastly more complex in the third ownership stage, marking the beginning of the family dynasty. As many cousins, in-laws and others without direct involvement in the business emerge as shareholders, new pressures arise. Allocation of corporate capital, and related issues such as dividend policy, debt levels, growth aspirations, and shareholder liquidity, become particularly important.

Shareholder differences emerge at this stage, if not sooner. With many shareholders lacking the intense involvement of their parents, the interests and identity of the family and the business often diverge at this stage. Family members who own stock but do not work in the company may wonder what is in it for them.

At the same time, questions may arise about the family's mission and role in perpetuating the business. Resolving family conflicts may become more difficult, with some members placing high value on family tradition and culture even as others grow restless and desire greater financial and professional freedom. Managing family members' ties with the business may become complex.

It is at this stage that many businesses confront a crisis. Some family members may demand to sell their shares, often just as the business itself requires new capital. Dissident shareholders may grow frustrated with the performance of their investment or the direction of the company. Increasingly, managing shareholder relations may divert management attention and drain valuable corporate resources. One way or another, these issues must be resolved. Feeling trapped or desperate, many family businesses owners respond by going public or otherwise divesting all or part of the company—no matter what their feelings may be about the value of perpetuating private ownership.

As best practices around family business governance become more widely known and understood, there is a trend toward development of formal family governance systems.

Board Insight

An increasing number of family businesses are developing formal, carefully structured family governance systems to manage the burgeoning array of ownership issues and to serve as a complement and interface to the board of directors.

Family ownership groups that invest in such an effort are typically able to consider a wider range of ownership options, as these family governance systems facilitate communication and better decision making. Well designed family governance systems enable owners to think through their options and arrive at an approach that makes the best sense for the family as a group, for the business going forward, and for the needs of the individual owners.

One path some families choose in order to reduce the complexities for later generations is to concentrate ownership in the hands of a smaller group of owners. In some cases, one branch of a family may buy out another. In others, families may split the business so that each branch can move forward on its own. In still others, the senior generation elects to pass stock down only to those members of the family who are actively participating in the business.

In a typical family, with two children as an average, third-generation businesses might logically have at least six owners, (two in the second generation and four in the third). Our survey showed that while 48 percent of respondents were in the third generation or beyond, only 34 percent had more than five owners. These figures suggest that some families are pursuing the option of concentrating ownership.

While concentrating ownership temporarily reduces the complexity of a large ownership base, it will need to be revisited again as new generations emerge. So, formal, carefully structured family and business governance are crucial even when a model of concentrating ownership is pursued.

Establishing a Family Council

A board with independent directors can be invaluable in helping solve the problems of family businesses in all stages. But a board of directors, no matter how experienced, cannot function effectively without a clear mandate of support from the shareholders. This mandate is best provided by an educated, cohesive shareholder group that has established a means for resolving conflict, articulating its interests, and educating itself on the business and the responsibilities of shareholders.

By the third generation of ownership, a carefully structured family council is often needed to provide education, resolve conflict, make important family decisions, and clarify the needs and expectations of shareholders. The family council can also create a sense of common purpose among family members and provide an opportunity for owners to participate outside the business itself. Perhaps most importantly, the family council allows the family to speak to the board with one voice.

Choose an Appropriate Structure

The family council can be structured in many ways, formally or informally. Many smaller families simply gather all members together for informal discussions. Others organize committees of family members to handle various matters and ask each committee to report annually to a meeting of the family as a whole. Some large families organize their councils like a representative government body. Either members of the council can be elected at large, or branches of the family can each select a delegate to the council.

Most family councils meet two to four times a year. Many combine business-related meetings and activities, such as plant visits or reports on business performance, with recreation in annual gatherings at a resort or hotel. Some invite family business consultants or other outside experts to these gatherings to deliver educational sessions or to facilitate family decision making. Larger families may engage a family business consultant to support the council on an ongoing basis and assist in planning council meetings.

Some families arrange meetings around the board's schedule to air family matters and views before directors meet. This gives the family a chance to communicate with the board. It also encourages family members who hold seats on the board to air personal feelings and opinions outside the boardroom in order to avoid consuming board time with matters more appropriate to the family council.

The Role of the Family Council

The family council's role is to find consensus on matters where the owners' wishes matter most, as well as to perform certain functions unique to the family. Ideally, the council can provide family members with a sense of identity and mission that transcends their role as mere financial stakeholders in a business. Some families establish bylaws to make the council's goals and membership criteria clear to everyone from the beginning. (See appendix 8 for sample family council bylaws.)

The typical family council faces a variety of important questions. What is the family's philosophy of doing business? What is its mission, both within and outside the company? How are members to resolve conflicts? How should family values be manifested in relation to the business?

Just as important is a long list of capital-related issues, such as dividend policy, liquidity policy, profit goals, growth goals, and the character and risk of the corporate investment portfolio. What businesses should we be in? Should we do startups? Where should we invest most heavily? Do we want to be highly leveraged? Do we want to invest in high-risk businesses?

The family council can also take responsibility for certain functions unique to the family. Preserving family traditions and values and educating family shareholders about the business are two important examples. Often, family education is required for family members to make informed decisions on such matters as appropriate debt, profit, growth and dividend levels for the business, the role of the shareholder, and other matters. A significant effort needs to be made to educate shareholders about the rights, responsibilities, and privileges that come with ownership.

Many family councils establish criteria and facilitate preparation of family members interested in serving on the board or in other governance roles. They also assure early exposure and education to good governance practices for younger family members.

Topics Important to the Family Council

- Allocation of capital; appropriate dividend, profit, debt, and reinvestment levels for the business
- Liquidity for shareholders
- Family business philosophy
- Family history and its role in the business
- Family culture and its role in the business
- Family values and their role in business strategy
- Performance of investments
- Estate planning by owners
- Family mission
- Family members' participation in the business
- Role in society; philanthropy, civic activities, politics

- Family responsibilities as business owners
- Family visibility in the public domain
- The role of the business in supporting family members' goals
- Education of family members in all these areas

The family council serves as a channel for communication to shareholders, in some cases through memos from the council to the shareholder group at large, in others through meetings, and also through newsletters or websites. In addition, some family councils take on various nonbusiness issues, such as philanthropy, family history, and family investments, among others. Committees formed to address these topics may report to a gathering of the whole family at family meetings or through other family communications channels.

Finally, the family council can cultivate among members a sense of cohesiveness and purpose completely separate from the goals of the business. Ideally, in a well-run business, the family council fosters among its members a sense of trust in managers and directors to oversee strategic objectives with only an appropriate level of involvement from shareholders.

In turn, shareholders' energy can be channeled into more productive activities, helping to transform unhappy family members into a collective source of energy and support for the family business. Equally important, the family council provides an outlet for contributions of family members whose skills and experience may not be ideally suited to participating in the business or on the board.

Some families with very large ownership groups, and also with a strong family social and development mission, carve out of the family council an *owners' council* or *owners' committee* to focus particularly on ownership and business board matters. By creating two bodies with unique missions, the family ensures that both ownership and social/educational agendas are attended to.

Tricky Issues in Family Business Governance

There are a number of challenging issues that must be navigated in establishing well-functioning family and business governance systems. For instance, how should independent directors interact with family shareholders? What boardroom information should be shared with all family shareholders? These issues are tricky because there is no simple answer. Even more complicating is the fact that the best answer for a particular family may change from generation to generation, requiring the family owners to revisit their decisions to make sure they are still appropriate in the current environment.

Among the tricky issues are the following:

Board selection/election process
1. How should family board members be selected:
   - By business competence, or
   - By at-large representation, or
   - By branch representation?
2. What is the best makeup of a nominating committee to recommend family directors?*
3. Who, for family representation, is eligible to serve on the board: in-laws, lawyer representatives, trustees?
4. Should family shareholders elect a proposed slate of family (or nonfamily) directors, or are competitive elections welcome?
5. Should it be public knowledge in the family which family candidates were not slated or elected?
6. Should the family vote be public or private?
7. Should the number of family board members be reduced when the family adds independent directors to the board? If so, how?

Boardroom culture
8. Should family members on the board speak as "one voice" of ownership to the board or express their individually conflicting views?
9. Among independent directors, how can the appropriate balance between family business empathy and capital markets dispassion be reached?*

10. Who should be welcome in the boardroom:
    - Nondirector family observers?
    - Next-generation associates in learning?
    - None of the above?
11. How much diversity and conflict is desirable in the boardroom?
12. How can directors know when being patient for a long-term view is really an excuse for poor managerial discipline?*
13. How can directors know whether a strong culture is a company strength or a constraint to company adaptability?*
14. How should independent directors be acculturated with the values, vision, heritage, and restrictions of the family?*

Board interface with family shareholders
15. How, and to what degree, should independent directors and family shareholders interact?
16. What boardroom information should be shared with all family shareholders?
17. What is the best role for the board chair in family shareholder relations?
18. How should family owners' satisfaction with the board be measured?

Board structure
19. What role might family members and family directors have on board committees?
    - Non-directors on board committees?
    - Family directors on compensation and/or audit committees?
20. How should the roles and membership of a holding company board be defined with regard to subsidiary boards?

Family director effectiveness
21. How should family members be prepared and developed for future board positions?
22. How should the performance of family board members be assessed? (What is the optimal process for development and/or evaluation? Who sees the results?)

Board compensation

23. Should independent and/or family directors receive equity-based or performance-based compensation?
24. Should family members on the board receive board fees—whether or not they are management directors?

In our surveys business families tell us the most challenging and relevant of these 24 "tricky issues" (designated with an asterisk) are numbers 2, 9, 12, 13, and 14, a majority of which deal with effective culture of the boardroom.

The Board Selection Process

By the time a family business has reached the third generation, a functioning board may already be in place. As evidenced by our survey, however, this is not always the case. Only 57 percent of respondents in the third generation or beyond had a board that meets at least three times a year. For those with such a board in place, slightly less than half have any independent directors; and only 19 percent have three or more independent directors. As the ownership group makes the decision to move to independent representation on the board, a number of challenges surface.

For some, the first challenge is restructuring family ownership participation on the board. In many cases it is not possible to add independent directors to the group of owners and management already on the board because the size would become unwieldy or because the owners on the board do not have the skills and experience to interact effectively with independent directors. Owners are then faced with the painful decision to eliminate some family representation on the board.

This blow may be cushioned by creating the family council in which members of the family who formerly sat on the board can find a home for their interests, talents, and contributions. Stressing the value independent directors will bring to the board may also help to cushion the blow to owners who must leave the board.

Finally, a dose of realism can be helpful in managing this transition. In all likelihood, if there are three or more owners on the board in the current generation, they should be well able to understand that there is no way that all owners will be able to sit on the board in the next generation. This means a selection process for owners to sit on the board is inevitable, and the sooner it can be implemented, the better.

There are a number of different models for selecting family shareholders to serve on the board. In designing an appropriate model, the ownership group must decide between a philosophy of merit and one of representation. If a merit-based philosophy is preferred, family directors must meet certain minimum criteria for serving as directors. These criteria may include education, business experience, and financial acumen. In extreme cases of a meritocracy, family directors are expected to meet the same requirements as independent directors, although this is very rare.

If the philosophy is one of representation, family directors are expected to represent the family's interests more than to bring specific skills to the boardroom. Even though they may not be required to bring the same skills as independent directors, the family still faces the challenge of defining qualifications for family directors—are in-laws eligible, is there a minimum age to serve, is ownership of voting shares required, should membership rotate periodically?

There are two types of representation—branch and at-large. In a branch model, seats are set aside for each family branch. The branch may nominate members to their seats for election by the full shareholder group or they may have the authority to elect them directly, with no input from other family branches. In an at-large model, seats are set aside for family directors and anyone who meets defined qualifications may be considered. In our experience, the most desirable model reflects at-large, rather than branch representation.

The second philosophical question in family board composition is that of selection versus election. In a selection model, the ownership group may handpick family directors who meet desired criteria. These criteria may relate to skills and experience or personality, position within the family (e.g., next generation), or other requirements. In an election model, family members run against each other, with those who receive the most votes becoming directors.

There is no single best model for all to choose, but the ownership group should clearly understand the implications of its choice. A meritocracy may yield more qualified directors, but it can exclude a large portion of the ownership base. Branch representation ensures broad involvement, but may lead to directors feeling they represent a constituency of shareholders rather than the whole. A selection model creates the opportunity for bias in whom is selected, whereas an election model can create opportunities for political battles to emerge. Families and their advisors usually work hard to try to develop a process whereby interested family members do not feel like "losers" if they are not selected or elected to serve on the board.

While not all boards that participated in our survey shared their model for selecting owner directors, the data from those who did showed a broad array of models. Of those who responded, 25 percent selected branch representatives, 25 percent used a nominating process, 20 percent an election process, and 30 percent selected only those owners who were employed in the business.

A third philosophical issue is raised by the board selection process, one that is at the root of other tricky issues—the philosophy around information sharing. The philosophy can lean more toward transparency or privacy. With respect to director selection, information sharing can be problematic in an election model. For example: Should the final tally of votes for candidates be shared with the full family or should only the winners be announced?

The benefit of transparency is that it tends to engender more trust; when information is not shared, suspicion follows. By contrast, the case for privacy is that feelings can be hurt when information is shared. Regardless of the choices that are made in designing the director selection process, a helpful rule of thumb is to enforce transparency of *process*. The process itself should be carefully debated and understood by all before an election takes place.

Boardroom Culture

Creating a positive boardroom culture poses another set of tricky issues, some more related to family directors, some to independent directors, and some to the board as a whole. As noted above, some of the most complicated issues are around boardroom culture. In selecting independent directors, owners must weigh the benefit of directors who are sympathetic to the nuances of family business versus those who take more of a dispassionate, value-maximizing mindset. There is no right or wrong; most likely an appropriate balance should be achieved, allowing the business to take advantage of the unique attributes of family ownership without sacrificing the focus on ensuring long-term business success.

To some extent, the desired mindset for directors will be set by the family's values—whether short-term versus long-term performance is valued, the family's appetite for risk and growth, whether flexibility is desired versus an adherence to legacy, among others. Adequately sharing the family culture and values with independent directors presents a challenge. While the owning family's values and priorities are important for independent directors, conveying this nuanced information to outsiders is not always easy to do.

Family directors who wear the combined hats of ownership and directorship as well as management can have a very strong impact on boardroom culture. Family directors can adopt the philosophy of representing the overall ownership group or their individual viewpoints. Family directors must determine whether they will reach consensus as a group and speak with one voice of "ownership" or whether they are free to voice individually conflicting views.

Board Insight

Conflict in the boardroom can be healthy if the diversity of viewpoints leads to constructive and creative discussions and, subsequently, to better decisions. However, if conflict results in stalemate or destroys relationships among directors, then it has gone too far.

To the extent that the family council can serve as a venue through which ownership consensus can be reached, the family board members can represent the consensus view.

Inviting third parties into the boardroom—management, nondirector owners, or paid advisors—can also impact the culture. While there are good reasons for expanding the audience in the board meeting, from bringing information and expertise to creating learning opportunities for future directors, the inclusion of outsiders can have a dramatic impact on the candor of conversations in the room.

Board Interface with Shareholders

The board plays a role outside as well as inside the boardroom. A separate set of issues is raised by the interaction of board members with shareholders.

A consistent flow of information from the board to family members is crucial in sustaining trust. Shareholders should receive board agendas and minutes as well as background on each director and information about each one's views. Some families send out information updates to all shareholders from two to six times a year.

Families can plan meetings in a way that encourages effective family-board interaction. Some hold family meetings before board meetings, airing ownership issues and, when appropriate, having a family member report to the board on ownership-related issues and concerns. Fireside talks, coffee hours, and social gatherings between family members and directors can help foster trust and give directors crucial information to help in making decisions that affect shareholder interests. Occasionally, individual directors might attend family gatherings as well. Optimally, these activities are held in an informal setting, helping give family members a sense of reassurance and comfort.

Some families delegate the task of finding consensus on major issues to a special task force that can select a representative to report the group's conclusions to the board. Others name a family ombudsman, whose job is to gather opinions from family members on crucial issues such as shareholder liquidity, the validity of the family mission statement, and so on. (A professional adviser can play the same role.)

In still other cases, the family council chairperson serves as a communications channel between family and board. Often the family council chair is invited to attend board meetings and writes a report to all shareholders on the board meeting.

While consistent communication is critical to a strong board-family relationship, two distinct challenges crop up—how to address confidential boardroom information, and how to deal with direct contact between shareholders and independent board members outside the boardroom.

With respect to information sharing, shareholders need to be educated about the importance of confidentiality concerning key strategic decisions. In some cases, the board may not be able to share all details of actions they are considering. For instance, if the company is considering an acquisition, it may not be appropriate to share this information with all shareholders in the investigatory stage, as the acquisition may have implications for the workforce of the acquired company as well as the shareholders' company. It may also effect the actions of competitors.

Similarly, sensitive information about pay and performance evaluations is best kept to a small audience. In some cases, independent directors, acting as a compensation committee, may be the only ones privy to information on CEO pay and performance. On the other hand, with more and more disclosure of compensation at public companies, family business CEOs and owners are becoming more comfortable with disclosure.

Another challenge arises when the communications flow in question is from shareholders to the board. Should owners feel free to contact independent directors with questions or concerns? While independent directors need to have a connection to the owners they serve, it is not healthy for owners to view these directors as the referees in a family fight. Raising concerns or asking questions is fine—asking directors to take a side or lobbying directors to sway their opinions is not.

Often, the board chair can serve as the interface between owners and the board. The family council chair may even play a role in managing relations between shareholders and the board. Whenever possible, the family council or the owner's council should be used as the venue for addressing shareholder concerns so that shareholders can present a united voice to the board, which can then act on shareholder objectives.

Councils can also provide a venue for shareholders to discuss their views about the board's effectiveness. Because the board evaluation process typically involves board members but not shareholders, there is not a clear-cut way for shareholders to voice their views on the board's performance other than through the annual election process. If there is a concern that the board is not performing to shareholders' expectations, a council may decide to survey or interview shareholders about their concerns or engage a consultant to evaluate the board's effectiveness and report to the shareholders.

Board Structure

The basics of board structure—size, mix of management, owners and independents, basic committee structure— have been addressed in earlier chapters. In later stage family businesses, more complicated board structure issues arise, particularly with respect to committees and subsidiary boards. Concerning committees, rules may need to be set that define who is eligible to serve on committee. Independent directors may be best suited for committees where issues related to family management are addressed—for example, compensation of key family executives. That said, some families want to have a family representative involved in setting compensation and evaluating performance of senior management, so this is not always the exclusive purview of independent directors.

As the number of family members in the business increases, the board may create a committee responsible for overseeing the development of family members in the business. Often referred to as a family human resources committee (FHRC), this group may oversee adherence to the employment policy, track individual family members' development, ensure that appropriate performance evaluations are conducted, and even coach or mentor next-generation family members in the business. The head of the human resources department may sit on the committee, even if not a board member. In fact, some families allow individuals who are not board members to serve on committees. In some families, owners participate on the governance committee, allowing owners' a window into the board evaluation process and input into the nomination of replacement directors.

Family businesses that have evolved into enterprises with many different companies or divisions are faced with other structural challenges. In the case of Canal Insurance, the family owners elected to create a separate board of directors for their real estate holdings, with experienced real estate professionals serving as independent directors. The owners of a large agriculture and real estate concern decided that the holding company level was the appropriate location for independent directors. At this company, subsidiaries are overseen by management boards, and senior management from one subsidiary may sit on the board of another to encourage learning across business units.

Board Insight

In considering board structure of multi-unit enterprises, owners need to think about where they could best use independent support in decision making, and the extent to which specialized board expertise would be valuable at a subsidiary level.

Owners must also ensure there is clear authority and accountability of subsidiary boards with respect to the holding company board. Authority and process for addressing topics that go across company lines must be addressed carefully, particularly in allocating capital across businesses.

While not a specific topic of this book, it is also worth noting that many later stage family businesses create separate boards for their family office or family philanthropy that incorporate independent directors. Often the owners' experience with independent directors on the corporate board opens their eyes to the value of objective, skilled executives in other board capacities.

Family Director Effectiveness

As previously mentioned, family directors who are not employees are prevalent on family business boards. Sixty percent of our survey respondents had nonemployee owners serving on their boards. Families choose different models for determining the skills sets and experience required of family directors, defining the role of family directors and selecting them. Regardless of the job description of the family director, family directors serve best if they are prepared for their role. Unfortunately, our research shows that less than 12 percent of those with nonemployee owners serving as directors have a formal process in place for preparing family directors.

Family councils can take an active role in preparing family members to be directors by holding education sessions on the roles and responsibilities of owners and boards, on basic business skills (such as reading financial statements), and on industry dynamics. In one family business, the CFO conducts a conference call each quarter for those family members interested in reviewing the quarterly financial statements and asking specific questions about the meaning of the statements. In another, a set of family owners is sent to a university-based family business seminar each year. When the owners return, they make a presentation to the family on what they learned as well as on ideas for improving their family business governance. Families may also develop a junior board, or shadow board, where next-generation members conduct a mock board meeting using the same agenda as the business board. Once family members begin serving on the board, evaluating their performance can be a complicated issue. If a formal board evaluation process is in place, as mentioned in a prior chapter, a peer evaluation can identify issues with family director performance. The challenge then becomes how to address these issues. One family shareholder raised an issue concerning privacy of board peer evaluation results: "Every year we elect our family directors to the board. What if one is not performing well? How would we know? I understand we don't want to embarrass family directors who are underperforming, but how can we ever solve the problem if we continue to elect those directors?"

Ideally, the chair should have a one-on-one conversation with a poorly performing director and agree upon a plan to address the issues identified. If the director understands the source of the problem, then this individual can work to address it or perhaps may even choose not to stand for election for the next term. The situation becomes more challenging if the director does not agree with the feedback.

However, allowing a poorly performing director to continue on the board can have a dramatic impact on the board's performance. In the case of one family business, the independent directors told the chairman they would not stand for reelection unless performance issues with a family director were addressed. They simply did not feel they could contribute unless that individual was removed.

Board Compensation

Determining how to compensate the board presents another set of tricky issues. Similar to many areas of our research, our results on director compensation demonstrate that a variety of models are used. With respect to overall compensation structure, 32 percent of those who paid directors compensated them with an annual retainer alone, 44 percent with quarterly meeting fees, and 18 percent with a combination of the two. A small percentage paid incentive compensation tied to company performance—4 percent paid some stock options or stock appreciation rights and 4 percent paid some other form of incentive compensation (almost always in addition to fees or a retainer).

Some families feel strongly that, when the company performs well, directors should be rewarded to acknowledge their participation and to create an incentive for them to drive business performance. Others feel that rewarding directors based on company performance can create conflicts of interest. Performance-based compensation may encourage directors to make decisions that drive short-term results but harm the company in the long run. Or, performance-based compensation can send the signal that bottom line financial performance is the only factor that should be considered in decision making, while the family may, in fact, have other objectives they are trying to achieve as well.

The disparity in compensation practices increases when considering who is paid for board service. Our research uncovered two models that were represented equally in the sample. One model is to pay independent directors but not family directors, while the other is to pay both family and independent directors the same amount. Most often, family directors who are also serving as managers are excluded from board compensation. Yet, the survey data showed that family directors who are managers were occasionally paid board fees.

Philosophies differ concerning remuneration for family board service. Some feel that serving as a director is a responsibility of ownership, one that need not be compensated. Others do not want to reward family directors with compensation because it creates an inequality between family members who serve on the board and those who do not. Still others feel it is important to compensate all directors the same amount, family and independent, to set the expectation that all provide an equal contribution to the board.

If independent directors are the only ones paid, there is a fear that a two-class system may emerge on the board in which independent directors are deemed the "real" directors and family directors are merely figureheads. Another problem can arise if family directors do not feel the responsibility to prepare and contribute because they are not compensated. In general we prefer nonemployed family members should be paid the same as independent directors—but not with shares or options.

Beyond the question of compensation structure, the amount of compensation is an area of considerable debate. Our survey shows a definite link between company size and director compensation. The average annual compensation of directors doubles when moving from companies of below $50 million in revenues to the $50–250 million category. It doubles again moving to the over $250 million bracket. That said, within the size categories, compensation varies widely. (For more information on compensation, refer to chapter 6.)

Designing the appropriate business and family governance systems presents a number of tricky issues to large business-owning families. To make the best decisions for their family, owners must be aware of the choices available to them and understand the implications of their choices. The family council can serve as a forum to discuss some of these issues. For others, the board may take the lead. Thinking through these issues in advance of designing the system will increase the likelihood of a well-performing system.

11

How You Can Contribute
As a Director

Few positions in business are as potentially intimate, challenging, or stimulating as that of the independent director. Effective board members may play roles ranging from statesman and sage to oracle, arbiter, friend, and confessor. The director may be a teacher one day and a critic the next, a source of emotional support one week and a philosopher shortly thereafter.

Service in the ambitious roles discussed in this book can raise some unfamiliar issues for directors. This chapter is addressed to them, and to those who may be considering invitations to serve. The chapter aims to help in evaluating board opportunities. It provides a framework for asking effective questions. It describes some appropriate ways to show interest in the business and to support the CEO. It also discusses some of the special ways family directors can contribute to the board.

What Should I Consider Before
Agreeing to Serve?

Many people say "yes" too quickly when asked to be a director. Good directors are precious and much in demand. When you are invited to serve, pause and consider whether the opportunity will be rewarding. Be sure you are comfortable with the leader, the owning family, their values, and the culture. The following are some pivotal questions we hear candidates ask themselves.

Do the CEO and the Owners
Really Want Help?

To offer a real opportunity to directors, the CEO should genuinely be seeking help and objective advice. There also must be consensus of the ownership group as to the value of a board.

"Some CEOs don't really want a board, and if they have one, they treat it sort of like a mushroom," says Ronald Taylor, the retired chief executive officer of DeVry, Inc., and a member of several boards. "Some do that in a very sophisticated way. They tie the board up in presentations and formalities."

The owners should be able to articulate a constructive purpose for the board. "The director has to ask herself whether the climate is right to make a contribution," says a much sought after director. "Is the board just window dressing for political or aesthetic purposes? Are the owners looking unrealistically for independent directors to settle a dispute within the group?"

Are Owners and Senior Management Candid
About the Company?

The parties responsible for conducting the director search should be forthcoming with information about the company's finances, culture, and strategy. "If they're not absolutely specific about the company's financial situation or competitive position, that worries me," says an experienced director. "If I become a member of the board, I really need to know those things to fulfill my responsibility."

Directors should have a high regard for the company's management and owners and should feel certain they are of the highest integrity before agreeing to serve. They should be proud of the association. They should feel comfortable that the company does not face any prohibitive threats of liability. They should also respect the corporate mission and philosophy.

Clayton Mathile, past CEO and chairman of IAMS Company, puts intellectual honesty at the top of his list of criteria. "If the CEO isn't willing to deal with the important and sensitive issues, I'm not there anymore," he says.

Will the Board Structure Permit Meaningful Input?

Many directors take steps to make sure the owners have established the right mission for the board; they want at all costs to avoid being treated as a rubber stamp. Directors also look for a certain critical mass of independent directors on the board. "I avoid the family tea party, where the wife and cousin and uncle are on the board and I'm the only outsider, making a nuisance of myself," says one experienced director, echoing a common complaint.

Can I Really Make a Contribution?

Sometimes, the director candidate is in a better position than the nominating committee to decide whether they have enough to offer.

If candidates have received a board prospectus, they can assess the extent to which the profile meets what they can bring to the table. In addition, it is helpful in conversations with the nominating committee and/or CEO to ask what skills and experience they think will be most helpful and what issues the board will likely address. Candidates can then assess the extent to which they can meet the board's needs.

Will I Benefit from the Experience?

In most situations, directors are happiest if they are able to gain something personally from the experience as well. Says one board recruiter, "I always ask candidates why they want to serve and what they think they will get out of the experience. If it is going to be a one-way street where candidates give but don't get much in return, they are unlikely to be happy in the long run."

Directors can benefit from boardroom experience in multiple ways—through exposure to a group of thoughtful peers, by digging into strategic issues that they may not have faced in their own businesses, or by serving a company that is tackling an issue they may envision having to deal with in the future. One CEO of a large second-generation family business was asked to join the board of another because of his experience with acquisitions. But, he was also interested in understanding how they had successfully built a family council to address ownership issues in the fourth generation.

Does It Look Like Fun?

The bottom line, directors agree, is that any board position should afford the board member pleasure, rewards, and an opportunity to learn.

An affinity with the business is an important prerequisite. "I wouldn't want to be involved as a director in any business that I wouldn't want to work for myself," says an experienced adviser. "If you can't see yourself in that business, don't accept." The personal chemistry should be right. "You have to like the CEO," he adds. "You have to want to help her and see her be successful. Basically, is the owning family one you hold in high regard?" The director should find other board members interesting and potentially stimulating as well.

Assuming the invitation meets all these criteria, the board member stands on the threshold of a provocative, challenging, and potentially gratifying experience. How can a director be most helpful? What advice do seasoned board members offer in supporting the CEO, showing interest in the business, and helping to resolve sensitive issues?

Ask Effective Questions

One of the greatest contributions a director can make is to identify, and sometimes challenge, deeply held assumptions on the part of management. This requires the board member to maintain an intellectual distance from management. To truly serve the company, the director must avoid slipping unconsciously into the same patterns of thinking as those who own and run the company. The most effective way for the director to accomplish this is to ask good questions. Inquiries that unearth assumptions and decision-making habits at work in the business can be enlightening for all concerned. On familiar topics, the right questions are often obvious to the director. Other times, even the most experienced directors rely, sometimes unconsciously, on a conceptual framework for questioning that enables them to examine unfamiliar subjects with rigor and discipline.

Following are lines of questioning that can be applied across multiple situations, even when the director does not have significant expertise on a topic. Note that none of these questions have "one right answer"—rather they are posed to stimulate substantive, thoughtful discussion.

What Process Was Used?

No director can address a management budget or plan with the same level of expertise and knowledge as the CEO or other managers who prepared it. But every director can raise the important questions about the process used to prepare the document. These "how" questions can expose inadequacies or strengths reveal in any plan.

"How did you arrive at this budget?" the board might ask the CEO. Was the process "top-down" or "bottom-up"? Is it a "wished-for" budget, or one that is made for the banks, or one set with a 50–50 chance of success? Is the budget sales-driven or financially driven? (That is, did you start by asking the sales group for revenue projections, or by asking your financial people what profit levels we should insist upon next year?) What are your assumptions about the economy, interest rates, and other variables? Did you develop contingency plans should any of those variables change?

Or, in the case of a pension or profit-sharing plan, the board might ask: "How did we choose the investment adviser? How did we decide on our investment philosophy and risk-taking posture? How did that affect our choice, and how did we convey those values to the adviser? How much choice among investment alternatives do we want to offer employees? How should we present the plan and communicate our investment philosophy to employees?"

What Trade-offs Are Involved?

Another major category of effective questioning aims to identify the risks or trade-offs inherent in any decision. If we make this choice, what side-effects will it have? Have you considered the impact on other constituencies, on the competition, on the community, and so on? Exploration of possible unintended consequences of important decisions is extremely valuable.

Pricing, dividends, and other strategic and financial decisions inevitably raise trade-off questions. What is the risk of holding down dividends to shareholders in order to keep our product prices down? If we force our suppliers to lower their prices so we can invest in research and development, what might we lose in terms of supplier reliability and loyalty? Should we hold down employee wages instead? If we do, what consequences will that have?

Compensation is another area rife with trade-offs. When presented with a compensation plan, the board might ask: "If we reward our star salespeople by basing incentives on individual performance, what impact will that have on the morale of the rest of the sales team or sales management? If we base our incentive plan on prevailing industry practice, how much will we lose in terms of attracting top-flight employees?"

Or, in the case of the company's philanthropic policy, the board might ask: "Are we missing an opportunity by failing to take into account employees' social or political concerns? Would we gain anything by tailoring our giving to reflect the nature of our business?" (In the case of a food company, for instance, donations to hunger-relief campaigns might have both social and public relations value.) "Would we benefit more by making only a few large, noteworthy donations or by dispersing our giving among many recipients?"

Evaluating trade-offs is related to one of the most important functions of the board—assessing and managing risk. In most cases, there are trade-offs, or risks, inherent in the decisions management makes. The job of the board is not to make these decisions for management but, rather, to ensure that management has accurately assessed the risks inherent in the choices made. We have observed in our work with boards that risk management is an area where boards acknowledge they do not dedicate enough attention.

Is Management Trapped by Habitual Thinking?

By the time management presents a topic to the board, they have usually worked it over hard and have sold themselves on the facts and logic. A great contribution is to search for disconfirming information: What would make the answer different? Also, it is valuable to examine whether a decision is made because of "sunk costs." (These are past costs that have already been incurred and cannot be recovered.)

A good question to ask is whether management would make the same decision given what they know today.

Is There a Contingency Plan?

One of a director's most helpful and provocative functions is scanning the horizon for unforeseen events or trends that could disrupt or damage the business. What broad social, economic, political, or market developments might affect our company? These contingency, or "what if," questions, are a useful antidote for many managers' natural tendency to focus too intensely inward on the business.

Questions might include: What if our biggest supplier enters our business? What if interest rates soar (or plunge)? What if the competitor in our industry gets really aggressive? What if a unionization movement develops in the company? How would we react if we were hit by bad publicity or a crisis of another kind?

Such questions from the board may seem nagging and worrisome, especially at first. But they serve a crucial function by encouraging the CEO to make a habit of contingency thinking—a discipline that can keep unpleasant surprises to a minimum. Exhibit 11.1 contains a further sampling of questions cited by experienced directors and CEOs as particularly helpful.

EXHIBIT 11.1: **Good Directors' Questions**

- How do our core competencies stack up to what will be required of the company to meet identified challenges and opportunities?
- Is the company meeting its potential? If not, what are the obstacles?
- What is our cost of capital, and is it appropriate to our strategy and mission?
- What is the value of the company? How is that value changing, and what does that tell us about company performance?

EXHIBIT 11.1: *Continued*

- Would the business be worth more in the hands of a different owner? If so, why?
- What are the top three strategic imperatives for the company, and how are operating decisions influenced by these imperatives?
- How are the strategies and goals referenced in the job descriptions and accountabilities of executive management?
- How well is senior management's compensation linked to company performance?
- What can be done to improve communications, teamwork, and decision making within the management team?
- What will ownership look like when the company is fully transitioned to the next generation?
- What are current owner expectations for the company, and how might they differ from those of the next generation?

Show an Interest in the Business

CEOs and family owners greatly appreciate directors whose interest in the business extends beyond the boardroom. Few gestures are more important in this regard than "doing one's homework." The chair who can count on directors preparing thoroughly for meetings has increased confidence in the board and tends to use it to the fullest extent.

Directors should also take advantage of invitations to visit company facilities and plants whenever time permits. Other valuables ways for directors to do their homework include visiting competitors, attending industry association events, or tracking competitors' websites. Reaching out to the CEO by sharing helpful information—from the news, seminars or conferences, etc.—will let the CEO know that directors are engaged in finding ways to improve the business. In addition, identifying areas to support the senior management team in areas of the directors' expertise can be extremely valuable.

One director suggested that the executive team go on a site visit at one of his facilities where some best practices were being implemented.

Research has shown that new directors bring an interest and enthusiasm to the business that may wane over time. Directors need to take stock, as their board tenure extends, to ensure they still have the energy and dedication required to be a good board member. If a director finds himself spending limited time preparing, or does not look forward to board meetings, it may be time to step down.

Support the CEO and Chair

A major function of directors is to support the CEO and chair whenever they can honestly do so, remembering that they must balance support with fiduciary oversight. This can be especially important for family businesses where the CEO is also an owner and may lack other objective sources of review and support. Here are some ways directors can be especially useful in this regard:

Help Monitor the Board's Performance

Individual directors can be of enormous help to the chair in reviewing and evaluating the board. While some boards hire an outside facilitator with responsibility for monitoring board performance, others conduct a written evaluation and still others rely on informal assessments.

Many chairs appreciate constructive feedback from individual directors on the board's performance, the CEO's use of the board, the agenda, informational materials, or other aspects of board operations. This input can be offered over lunch, in other private sessions, or during the board meeting if appropriate. As previously discussed, some chairmen find it helpful to set aside time during one board meeting each year for directors to appraise the board's performance and make suggestions.

Help the Chair Make the Best Use of the Board

Some chairs, especially those who lack experience with independent directors, make mistakes in dealing with their boards. Failing to keep directors informed, failing to consult with the board, and other tactical errors can lessen the board's effectiveness and directors' morale.

Many directors use such mistakes as opportunities to coach the chair in the proper role of the board. One experienced director points out that if a CEO surprises the board with an agreed-upon acquisition or some other *fait accompli*, directors might say, "Look, we'd like to know more about this. Next time, why don't you use us before you decide? Let us help you ask the right questions."

In other cases, CEOs may try to dodge problems. If the chair or CEO starts canceling board meetings or talks sports instead of business, "that tells me there's a problem," the aforementioned director says. The director's role in such a situation, he says, is to "talk with the CEO and figure out a way to do so that isn't threatening."

Defer Decisions When Appropriate

Most matters that come before the board do not have to be decided overnight. The boardroom is more hospitable than most business settings when it comes to deferring judgment. In fact, many issues become easier to resolve if allowed to rest between board meetings. Often, a board's deferral of a decision can be helpful to the CEO in deflecting shareholder pressure or in simply sanctioning a reflection period to allow all concerned to think things over.

Offer Sensitive Advice in Private

Directors often have insights into sensitive business matters that cannot be addressed in the boardroom. Board members who enjoy a trusting relationship with the chair or CEO can sometimes address these matters over lunch, on the golf course, or in another informal, relaxed setting.

One CEO was squelching the efforts of his designated successor—his son—without realizing it. The CEO was proud of the young man and praised him privately to the board. But whenever the son reported to directors on his areas of responsibility, the CEO unconsciously fell into his old patterns as a father, preempting normal board discussion with pointed criticism that clearly undermined the young man's morale.

Sensing a problem that could damage the business, a long-time director asked the CEO out for a round of golf. "Look, Pete," he said, "I'd like to offer an observation that I think will be helpful. You said something to John the other day in our meeting that might be a little deflating to him, and I've noticed you've done that before, too. You might want to think about the effect that's going to have on his self-confidence and his ability to run the business someday. He takes tough feedback from us well, but, as you are his father, whom he admires, he takes it harder."

The CEO was shaken but accepted the suggestion and thought it over. To his credit, he was able to change his patterns of boardroom behavior and begin treating his son in a more conscientious manner.

The Importance of Empathy

Working with an aggressive, candid board can be difficult for the CEO, particularly for the business leader who is unaccustomed to giving up control or being held accountable. Often, the observant director can help with an empathic remark, such as, "I haven't got all this figured out in my own business either, Joan."

A simple acknowledgement may soothe the CEO who is smarting from board criticism. "I guess it's our day to beat up on you, Mike," a director might say. Or, "How does it feel to get picked on by a bunch of outsiders who don't know your business as well as you?"

A note of sympathetic humor can also provide a healing touch. When one CEO sought his directors' reactions to his idea of promoting an insider to a key post, he was chagrined at their negative response. "Everybody has to go outside from time to time," one director told the CEO.

Seeing the disappointment on the CEO's face, another board member remarked, "And every single time I've done it, it's been a pain!" The tension in the room eased amid a burst of laughter and the CEO visibly relaxed.

Avoid Putting the CEO on the Defensive

Whenever possible, the director should avoid making remarks so critical of the CEO that they lack productive impact.

One director recalls a situation in which a CEO and his investment manager were proudly describing to the board some successful individual stock picks they had made on behalf of the company pension plan. Notably missing, though, was an explanation of the team's overall investment philosophy or goals.

"I came driving in from left field and said, 'Wait a minute! What's the strategy?'" the director recalls. The discussion spun off the tracks as the CEO defended his choices and the director knew he had made a mistake. "Great ideas tend to follow from a constructive approach, but I put the guy on the defensive," he says. "You shouldn't put people who have worked hard on something in the position of feeling threatened by your 'genius question.'"

Resist Boardroom Competition

Some boards, especially at first, have one member who is more outspoken than others. This can make other members feel they should step up their own contributions. In the worst case, it can create an escalating contest among directors trying to outdo each other.

Many directors find it helpful to remember that inequities among board members' contributions tend to even out over time as a variety of issues arise and members grow accustomed to working as a group. In a council of peers, competition should be nonexistent. No one should feel a need to prove anything; instead, all should feel free to offer questions, ideas, and suggestions at their own individual pace.

Ease Needed Board Transitions

Directors who become too attached to their board seats can cause the owners and chairman deep discomfort. Few situations are more awkward for the chairman than dealing with a director's reluctance to resign or retire when asked. Some retain board members long beyond their usefulness, simply to avoid hurting the feelings of these longtime associates and friends.

The effective director is mindful of the board's role as a resource that must be tailored to the changing needs of the CEO and the business, and tries to act accordingly. When one young owner first took over as CEO of the family business, a valued independent director took him aside. With the previous CEO retiring, the director said, "I've given some thought to the idea that maybe it's time for me to go, too." The CEO was stunned: "I dropped my jaw," he says, and quickly set about persuading the director to stay.

Gratefully, the director agreed. "He just wanted to hear that I wanted him," the CEO says with appreciation. "He wanted to know that I believed he could contribute."

Seek One Value-added Idea Per Meeting

The best directors we have known consistently contribute one valuable idea each meeting, sometimes more. Upon study, we have learned these excellent directors really think about the agenda, the materials, and give serious reflection for days before the meeting. They use this time to think about how they can best use their skills and experience to add value to the planned discussions.

Special Issues for Independent Directors of Family-owned Businesses

Often, directors are asked to serve family businesses with large, diverse ownership base. These board members face some special challenges, particularly if the shareholder group is discontented or divided.

One is to help shareholders recognize that certain issues are inherent in family businesses. While the owners may not see—or wish to see—the problems clearly, an effective director can often help the family address and resolve them. "If there's a family in there running things, part of the mission of the board is to help the family make it together," a committed director says.

Periodic social gatherings or fireside chats with shareholders can help foster good relations with family members and provide directors with the information they need to understand the family-business dynamics. Some of the issues directors may face in this context are highlighted below.

Drawing the Line Between Family and
Business Matters

One of the most sensitive matters is helping the owners balance family needs and the demands of running a healthy business. As the family business evolves over succeeding

generations, owners need to find an outlet for family opinions and emotions, legacy thinking, and even conflicts.

As noted earlier, family gatherings or a family council
can serve this need. For families who have not developed an
appropriate venue for addressing family issues, independent
directors can encourage the family to separate family and
business issues by developing a place and method for dealing
with them.

Board Insight

Even when families have developed family governance, independent board members may need to reinforce the separation of family and business issues and recommend that issues
raised in the boardroom be posed to the family instead.

As one nonfamily board chair commented, "If something
comes up in the board room that owners need to discuss, I
tell them they need to take it to the family."

One family, for instance, agonized over the impending
divorce of a son who was the designated successor to his father.
When the father's hurt feelings and disappointment began
interfering with his business dealings with his son, directors
were uniquely able to define the issue. "Look, you've got to
draw the line here" between business and personal matters,
one board member told the father. "I'm not here to tell you
where the line is, but you have to decide. If you're going to
throw your son out over a divorce you don't like, that's one
thing. But if you want him in the company, you've got to try
to separate your personal feelings from business matters."

Serving As a Lightning Rod

Occasionally, the director can calm family conflict by listening to unhappy shareholders and guiding them toward an
appropriate resolution. But directors should be extremely

cautious in this regard. No director should become the emotional dumping ground or leaning post for a disgruntled shareholder. In most cases, the director should seek ways to bring a shareholder's complaints out in the open so they can be aired and resolved in an appropriate way. This protects the director from being caught in the middle of a family triangle, acting as an intermediary between family members.

In businesses with large shareholder groups, clarifying the appropriate channels for voicing shareholder concerns can become important. Some families designate the family council leader as the point person for shareholders. Others may choose the board chair. Regardless, it is helpful to outline a clear process and enforce it with shareholders. As one independent board member commented, "I am happy to hear from family shareholders, but if they have a specific issue, with the treatment of a family employee for instance, I let them know that they should contact the head of the family council who serves as the clearinghouse for shareholder concerns."

Taking Sides in a Family Dispute

Directors should avoid taking sides in a family disagreement. Aligning oneself with a faction of the family almost invariably ends the board member's usefulness to the business. In all cases, directors should make clear that they represent the interests of all stakeholders and all shareholders, not just one constituency, and that the director's principal concern is business policy and performance. In some cases, directors may recommend bringing in another outside adviser, such as a compensation expert or family-business consultant, to help resolve disputes.

Returning Issues to the Family for Resolution

Some thorny issues wind up with the board when, instead, they should be thrashed out by the family. A director presented with a dividend dispute, for instance, might rightly ask the family to decide on desired debt and reinvestment levels of the business. Once the family reaches consensus on that issue, their input can be provided to the board, where directors can balance this input with the needs of the business. Directors can often be helpful by providing "benchmarking data" from their own experience to help reach the best answer.

Anticipating Future Family-related Business Issues

Part of the director's role in the family business is to help anticipate future family-related business issues. Early in their board terms, directors should take stock of certain critical aspects of family-business health. Here is a sampling of questions the director might consider:

- Is the family articulating its philosophy and values and ownership vision for the business and putting them into effect?
- How strong is the family consensus on such key issues as dividends, growth, profit performance, and shareholder liquidity?
- How much capital will be needed to satisfy shareholders' future needs and demands?
- What will ownership and leadership succession look like for the next generation?
- Is the next generation being actively prepared?
- Are any other issues looming that could fragment the shareholder base?
- If the shareholder base is already fragmented, are extreme actions needed, such as management buyout, a public sale of stock, or a buyout of the dissident shareholders?

Once directors understand the dynamics of the family business, they can be of great help in framing prospective issues—often by asking the "what-if" kind of questions described earlier in this chapter.

While these can be difficult issues, the director can comfort the owners by pointing out that they are nearly universal in family businesses. "These are problems and questions that every owner has to expect," directors might tell the ownership group. "Businesses change over time, and there's no way you're going to look ten or 20 years from now the same way you look now. Some very normal changes have to occur."

Supporting Succession and Family Employee Development

A Family Human Resources Committee that includes one or two independent directors can be extremely valuable in planning and assessing next-generation career development and performance. If such a committee is not in place, independent directors may encourage the owners to create a mechanism for next-generation development. When board members are present for a succession event, a "Succession Task Force" can help prepare for it, guiding the timeline and anticipating issues of organization, compensation, transition, and public relations.

Unique Roles for Family Directors

Family-member directors are prevalent on family business boards. Just as independent directors make unique and valuable contributions, family directors fill a special role. Family directors can ensure continuity of vision and values across the family and business, serve as a channel for communication back to shareholders, educate new directors on the business history and values, and at times even play a role in giving directors a "heads up" on contentious shareholder issues before they surface at the board level. Family directors also provide assurance to the broader shareholder base that the independent directors are adding value to the governance process as first-hand observers in the board room.

While family members serving as directors can provide a valuable link to shareholders, it is crucial that they view themselves as representatives of the overall shareholder group in support of business continuity, as opposed to being representatives of their own interests or those of their family constituency. Family directors can often find themselves challenged by the multiple hats they must wear in the boardroom. For instance, it can be difficult to hear board members question the performance of a family member in management who may also be a close relative, a father, or favorite nephew. Family directors must do their best to keep family relationships out of the board decision-making process. As with independent directors, family directors must be careful to maintain their focus on business policy and performance.

Resources for All Directors

Directors, both owners and independent directors, should not hesitate to reach out for advice, information, and support from various sources. The company's general counsel can be helpful to directors in understanding their legal duties. *The Corporate Director's Guidebook*, published by the American Bar Association, is another resource that provides useful information on board responsibilities. The National Association of Corporate Directors also publishes newsletters and organizes membership programs for directors (see www.nacdonline.org).

To learn more about the business, some directors like to attend industry seminars or conventions. Board members might also ask the CEO for industry-wide performance data and financial ratios to help in reviewing the company's performance. A subscription to industry trade magazines can be helpful. Other resources, such as consultants on compensation, HR, or strategy may be needed from time to time to provide a perspective independent of management.

Nor should directors neglect one another as resources. Many board members discuss board issues informally to test their perceptions and gather feedback on complex issues.

To conclude, serving as an effective director can raise some challenging and unfamiliar issues, even for experienced executives, entrepreneurs, and business owners. Directors should evaluate board invitations carefully before agreeing to serve. The integrity and sincerity of the owners and management, and the potential for making a real contribution are the essential factors a candidate should consider.

Raising good questions is a central role of the director. While no one can possibly know as much about any business as the CEO and senior management, many board members rely, sometimes unconsciously, on a strong conceptual framework for effective questioning. This approach helps improve the quality of company decision making by examining the process used to make a decision, the trade-offs involved, and the contingencies that might affect that decision. These "how," "who's hurt," and "what-if" questions can encourage the CEO to internalize a rigorous, disciplined approach to decision making of all kinds.

Directors can provide valuable support to the chair in several subtle but important ways. They can help monitor board performance and encourage optimal use of the board. Directors can provide empathic support to the CEO in difficult situations. They can also encourage productive discussions by resisting any urge to compete with other directors or to put the CEO on the defensive.

Directors in family businesses face some special challenges. Often, they can help shareholders decide where to draw the line between family and business issues. They can serve as lightning rods in shareholder disputes, helping channel differences of opinion to the proper forum. And they can help the ownership group anticipate future issues that might affect the welfare and survival of the family business.

12

Our Call to Action

From our pioneering studies and decades of personal experience, we are convinced that an active board with independent directors is the single greatest step for family business success and continuity. As we have stressed throughout, an active board is one that meets at least three times per year; and an independent board is one that includes at least three objective outsiders. This powerful combination creates a board that is a unique resource in many ways.

The active, independent board is a catalyst, a facilitator, a guide, and a comfort for the trials of succession planning. Preserving the continuity of your enterprise is their number-one role.

To ensure long-term business success the board will urge that an emergency succession plan be in place. It will stimulate an ownership and leadership vision that provides the framework for the choice of leaders and governors for the future. It will assist in the preparation and assessment and development of successor candidates—working patiently and persistently for the ultimate selections to be self-evident and embraced by all.

The board will support and coach the new leaders and the next generation of owners. It will counsel the owning family on how to communicate succession plans to all stakeholders and how to adapt the organization and culture for the new leadership.

Beyond succession, the independent directors on the board are the best possible source of questions, challenges, and ideas for the business's strategy. They know and respect the family's values. They test assumptions, bring deep personal experience, and provide supportive brainstorming. They also assure that strategic performance measures are in place, and that there is disciplined implementation and execution.

An active, independent board is also a special resource to the owning family. The boardroom is a trusted forum in which to address sensitive topics, from compensation to redemption policies. The independent directors will promote the development of a family plan and family meetings. They will affirm what are "normal family business challenges," and they will champion the special advantages of the family firm and of family unity and commitment.

An effective board provides support, transparency, accountability, counsel, and confidence. It offers hope when things are most difficult; it challenges the status quo when things seem most comfortable. Most fundamentally the independent directors respect the owning family's dream; and they will also nurture the decision to let go of the family business if that is what is best for all.

You cannot hire such help. Good independent directors serve because they believe in you, and they believe that family businesses matter in our society. They also serve because you challenge them with meaningful agendas, and you have an open mind to their ideas.

Why, then, from our studies, do only one-third of family owned businesses take advantage of this invaluable resource? We find two basic reasons.

First, business owners do not imagine this resource is possible. "Why would someone, with more experience than we, and held in such high respect by so many others, be interested and available to us?" We hope the data and real examples provided in this book overcome that misperception. This sort of doubt, coupled with personal modesty, accounts for much of the hesitation business owners have about building a strong board.

Think about that concern from a different point of view: What if a business-owning family came to you and said it was facing some difficult challenges to long-term continuity, that it was committed to learning and governing, that it wanted to preserve and extend its values-based culture, and that the family leaders knew you could really help them. Even though it might take several days a year of your scarce time, would you not be greatly tempted to say, "Yes, I'd like to try to be helpful to you." (Besides, you know you would find the strategic think-tank environment that good boards provide stimulating—even for your own business.)

We cannot promise miracles, of course, and we know making good boards work takes time and thought. But with great confidence we say that 19 out of 20 boards developed as we have outlined in this book will add tremendous value. We know from our surveys that every family business with an independent board finds it valuable, most of them very valuable. We know that, if properly recruited, only one director per ten man-years will eventually not measure up and need to be replaced. Even this is not an insurmountable challenge as refreshing your board is valuable in any case.

We hope we have been convincing that, with the assistance of a family business consultant, or an empathetic search firm, or of a passionate family task force, your company can and will find excellent director candidates. We have attempted to help you understand how to identify and recruit excellent, relevant candidates.

We also hope we have provided examples and suggestions on how to make the boardroom optimally effective. Having committed, caring talent together for 20–40 hours per year (four to five half- to full-day meetings) is too precious to waste. It starts with asking the board important, critical, questions. Effective chairs identify two or three questions per board meeting and then work, foremost, as facilitators of a rich dialogue. That means even more questions: What has been your experience? How can we test that idea? How can we be sure? What do you think is the cause? What are the disadvantages of this idea? What might disconfirm our assumptions? How will we know if we are succeeding? What do you think are the next steps? What are the pros and cons of taking this course of action?

Some business leaders let someone else facilitate the meetings so they can spend 100 percent of their time listening and participating. Outside help can also be valuable in designing effective, efficient information for the board members, and to manage effective communications about the board to the organization and other stakeholders.

We know that your other stakeholders—employees, customers, bankers, etc.—are reassured and impressed if you have an excellent board. After all, having one is clearly an expression of open-mindedness and accountability and commitment to long-term continuity.

Another reservation we hear, from modesty, is: "I want the benefits of a good board, but I want to fix some things first." A natural thought. But we have found that the board will help "fix things" faster and better so that the other benefits can come faster and better.

The role and value of effective corporate governance has been studied for years, and from many hundreds of these surveys we know people proclaim the following key benefits from a board:

1. Help the CEO with difficult or important decisions.
2. Aid in the continuity of the enterprise.
3. Be there for a crisis.

There are, of course, the added benefits of networking, reputation, holding professional service providers more accountable, and providing discipline to top management.

While these benefits are important on their own, for business-owning families the case for an active, independent board is even more compelling. For wise, respected counselors to certify the successor adds a special a confidence and legitimacy to that successor. In the case of sibling co-owners, the most vulnerable ownership structure, the independent board offers support and oversight. For family firms with nonemployed cousin owners, the independent directors' objectivity and sense of fair play will help to effectively address some of the common challenges that arise in such situations.

While we have sung the praises of the independent director a great deal in this book, there is one other key ingredient to excellent family business governance: the family members who also serve on the board. We were quite surprised in our research to find that 60 percent of family firms have *nonemployed* family owners on their boards. That said, we were less surprised to find that only 20 percent family business boards provide deliberate preparations and development programs for family directors.

Here lies a great opportunity. Any chance a business-owning family has to invest in the development of family members should be seized with relish. The family members benefit, the board benefits, the family business benefits. The example that is set informs the next generation that serving on the board is more an important responsibility than an entitlement.

How to prepare and educate directors is an important question, one in which we hope family owners will invest the needed time and energy. We have given some good pointers to get started in this book, but there is always more to learn.

We have professed in other writings by The Family Business Consulting Group that *perpetuating the family business is the ultimate management challenge.* We believe an active, independent board is the single greatest resource for success.

And we have often argued for the "competitive strategic advantages" and superior performance of family business ownership. We know that good governance is the key ingredient to releasing and maximizing the benefits of unconventional strategy, contrarian thinking, and a values–based culture. Good governance provides the checks and balances that give management with the confidence to do the unusual.

We are also keen advocates of the benefits of family enterprise in our society. We know family firms create jobs and are very generous and faithful to their communities. We know that the dream of family ownership succession motivates the commitment to long-term thinking and stability of purpose and culture. An active, independent board not only helps achieve these ideals, but also conveys to society that family-owned firms are transparent, accountable, progressive, and committed to ethical principles.

Well-governed family-owned firms provide a needed model of enterprise. We salute you for your commitment to this goal and are eager to hear more from the trenches.

Please share your experiences and explore your questions with us and with other business-owning families on the blog "Family Education, Thoughts and Wisdom," which can be found at http://familybusinessconsultinggroup.com.

Appendix I

Example Board Prospectus

Overview

XYZ Company seeks to expand its board of directors to help the company navigate the strategic challenges faced by the media industry and to transition the business to the next generation of family ownership. Headquartered in Anytown, U.S.A., XYZ is a diversified media company, with operations in radio, television, and newspaper publishing. Technology and consumer tastes have significantly changed the media industry, challenging the company with the need to evaluate strategic options for the future. At the same time, XYZ is transitioning from the second to the third generation of family ownership. Through this transition, the board will ensure that the interests of owners who are neither employed by the business nor serving on the board are well represented.

XYZ seeks two individuals who meet the criteria specified in this prospectus to join the board of directors.

Business Summary

XYZ ("the Company") was founded in 1950 when John Anderson and Bill Cooper launched the *Anytown USA Gazette*. The Gazette is still the flagship property, and family members have held the editor and publisher positions at the newspaper for three generations. The Company expanded into radio 20 years later with the acquisition of its first station. The Company has continued to grow through acquisitions. Today, the Company publishes ten papers, has four television stations, and five radio stations, all in the western United States. For more information on the Company, see our website at www.xyzmedia.com.

XYZ is the dominant player in all markets it serves. The Company prides itself on its staff of knowledgeable, entrepreneurial operators, who are given significant discretion in running local operations. The Company is financially stable and well-capitalized.

The owners and management of XYZ have articulated the Company's values, vision, and strategic objectives to serve as a guide for the future.

Core values:

Company vision:

Strategic objectives:

XYZ management team is led by the third-generation president and CEO, Jeff Anderson. Joe Cooper, second generation, serves as chairman of the board. The senior management team consists of:

The business is owned by second and third generation descendents of the founders. No family member holds a controlling interest.

Board of Directors

Need for a Board

XYZ is currently overseen by an active board composed of family manager/shareholders. As the business model in traditional and new media continues to evolve, the owners and management value the infusion of an independent perspective and ideas from other industries into strategic decision making. The addition of independent directors will further clarify and segregate the role of management and ownership. Owners see the addition of independent directors as the next phase in the evolution of the board.

As the Company transitions from a second-generation business—in which all family members participated in management and were on the board—to a third-generation business with several shareholders who are not involved, the oversight provided by an independent board is valued. Owners expect directors to consider and represent the owners' interests, formulate and monitor the long-term strategic agenda, ensure effective decision-making processes within the business, and serve as advisers to the CEO.

Board Responsibilities

XYZ seeks seasoned board members who will have an immediate impact on the business. Board members are expected to share their insights and ideas, and to push and question management thinking. A culture of open discussion and debate is encouraged.

Specific responsibilities of the board include:

- Review Company performance and identify issues that need to be addressed.
- Hold management accountable to achieving strategic, operating, and financial objectives.
- Evaluate strategic alternatives, including acquisitions and divestitures, diversification opportunities, and new revenue streams.
- Review, evaluate and approve the strategic plan.
- Review and approve operating and capital budgets. Make capital allocation decisions across various enterprises
- Bring new ideas to the table, challenge management thinking, and share insights from other industries.
- Ensure that owners clarify their vision and objectives in order to provide context for board decision making.
- Evaluate senior management performance and approve compensation. Ensure a strong management team is in place.
- Enforce appropriate board role and responsibilities, meeting agenda, preparation, facilitation, and evaluation to ensure the board operates effectively.

Board Structure and Commitment

The board is currently comprised of the CEO, two owners in senior management positions and two nonemployed owners. The owners would like to add three independent directors to join these owners.

The board meets five times per year, for four quarterly meetings and a strategic planning and budget approval meeting in December. All meetings are held in Anytown.

Directors will stand annually for election at the April shareholder meeting. Owners hope board members will commit for a minimum of two to three years at outset, subject to annual approval by shareholders.

Directors will be paid $25,000 annually. Expenses related to board work will be reimbursed. Compensation will be in the form of a $10,000 annual retainer and $3,000 per meeting fees.

The Company provides sufficient D&O insurance coverage in addition to the indemnification through its corporate bylaws and articles of incorporation.

Director Profile

XYZ seeks to attract candidates who have demonstrated success in their fields and have held senior management roles in, or have advised, businesses that match or exceed the size and complexity of ABC. Candidates should be good communicators with strong character and integrity, possess sound strategic thinking and problem-solving skills, and the ability to effect change. Candidates are expected to have an immediate impact, study our issues, and voice their opinions.

Specific experience and skills valuable to the Company include:

- Reinventing a business in which the traditional business model has become obsolete or has changed significantly (e.g., identifying new revenue streams, leveraging core competencies in new ways).
- Financial acumen—the ability to assess financial performance and the financial impact of strategic alternatives, make capital allocation decisions, and evaluate large financial transactions.
- Experience in a consumer goods or services business with a strong analytical, market-driven focus.

- Exposure to media beneficial, with preference for cable and online media.
- Experience sustaining growth over a long period of time (acquisitions integration experience beneficial).
- Board service for companies or nonprofits that match or exceed the size and complexity of ABC.
- Understanding and appreciation of dynamics that drive family-owned businesses.

Appendix 2

Committee Responsibilities

Audit Committee Responsibilities

1. Recommend and review selection of outside auditors.
2. Assure the efficient completion of internal and external audits.
3. Review and approve annual internal and external audit procedures, including the methodology and areas of audit and revisions to the annual report.
4. Review and approve accounting, legal, and financial policies.
5. Ensure methods are in place for identifying and investigating potential fraud.
6. Review financial statements before they are presented to the full board.
7. Ensure shareholders receive adequate financial information from the Company.

Compensation Committee Responsibilities

1. Supervise the design and implementation of policies related to compensation, performance evaluation, employee development, and retirement.
2. Approve the personal development plans for senior-level executives.
3. Approve annual salary increases for senior-level executives.

4. Conduct a formal performance evaluation of the CEO.
5. Review performance evaluations of senior-level executives.
6. Oversee the development of succession plans for senior-level management.
7. Propose programs for professional development for shareholders.

Governance Committee Responsibilities

1. Identify and recommend independent director candidates.
2. Recommend candidates for board officer positions and board committee membership.
3. Develop a succession plan for the board chair.
4. Make recommendations to the shareholder assembly of appropriate compensation levels for board members.
5. Coordinate the annual board-evaluation process.
6. Develop and recommend long-term board goals for approval by the full board.
7. Ensure that all committees have established objectives and charters.
8. Oversee the board orientation process for new board members.
9. Assure that a code of ethics guides business and director conduct.

Audit Committee of the Board of Directors Charter

Committee Structure

The Audit Committee shall be composed of directors who are independent of the management of the corporation and are free of any relationship that, in the opinion of the board of directors, would interfere with their exercise of independent judgment as a committee member. Ex-officio members of the Audit Committee may also be appointed by the board of directors.

Mission

The Audit Committee shall provide assistance to the board of directors in fulfilling its responsibility to the shareholders with regard to corporate accounting, reporting practices of the company, and the quality and integrity of financial reports of the company. In so doing, it is the responsibility of the Audit Committee to maintain free and open means of communication between the board of directors, the independent auditors, the internal auditors, and the financial management of the company.

Responsibilities

In carrying out its responsibilities, the Audit Committee believes its policies and procedures should remain flexible, in order to best respond to changing conditions and to ensure that the company accounting and reporting practices are in accordance with all the requirements of accepted standards.

In carrying out its responsibilities, the Audit Committee shall:

- Review management's selection of the independent auditor.
- Meet with the independent auditors and financial management of the company to review both the scope of the proposed audit for the coming year and the audit procedures to be utilized. At the conclusion of the audit, the Audit Committee shall review the audit findings, comments, and recommendations with the board of directors.
- Review with the independent auditors, the company's internal auditor, and financial and accounting personnel, the adequacy and effectiveness of the accounting and financial controls of the company, and elicit any recommendations for the improvement of such internal-control procedures or particular areas where new or more detailed controls or procedures are desirable. Particular emphasis should be given to the adequacy of such internal controls to expose any payments, transactions, or procedures that might be deemed illegal or otherwise improper
- Periodically review company policy statements related to financial reporting, controls, and risk management to assure their appropriateness and consistency with company philosophy.
- Review with management and the independent auditors the financial statements contained in the annual report to shareholders to determine that the independent auditors are satisfied with the disclosure and content of the financial

statements to be presented to the shareholders. Any changes in accounting principles should be reviewed.

- Review the competency of accounting and financial personnel as well as succession plans within this group.
- Submit the minutes of all meetings of the audit committee to the board of directors and formally report to the board at least semiannually on pre- and post-audit matters.
- Investigate any matter brought to the Audit Committee's attention within the scope of its duties, with the power to retain outside counsel for this purpose if, in its judgment, such action is appropriate.

Compensation Committee of the Board of Directors Charter

Committee Structure

The Compensation Committee shall be appointed by the chairman of the board and shall consist of two outside directors and a chairperson selected by the chairman.

Mission

The Compensation Committee shall establish and administer executive compensation policies that are aligned with the company's strategic business objectives. In their deliberations, the committee will consider guiding principles for executive compensation as provided by ownership as well as other appropriate standards of professional compensation and performance management.

Responsibilities

The Compensation Committee shall meet at least annually and shall be responsible for the following:

- Review and approve the company's compensation philosophy and guidelines as they apply to executive officers.
- Conduct an annual performance evaluation of the CEO and review the CEO's performance evaluations of his direct reports

- Make recommendations to the board of directors regarding the compensation of the company's key executive officers.
- Periodically review and recommend appropriate changes to the company's overall compensation and performance-management policies.
- Periodically review the content and performance of the company's pension and profit sharing plans.
- Monitor the company's adherence to shareholder guidelines on compensation.
- Formulate and monitor succession plans for the key executive officers of the company.
- Submit the minutes of all meetings of the Compensation Committee to the board of directors.

Appendix 3

Family Director Qualifications and Nominating Process

Family Directors—Nomination Process

1. The Family Council, or if so designated, a subcommittee of the Family Council, invites recommendations, including self-recommendations for nominees to serve on the board of directors. Those who choose to pursue a Family Council nomination will present to the Family Council their reasons for requesting consideration and their background. Individual Family Council members who are recommended will recuse themselves from the nomination process; step 2 below.

2. The Family Council, using pre-established criteria (attached), and with input from the CEO regarding the needs of the business, decides on nominees and presents their nomination to the Board of Directors Development Committee. Potential candidates must be direct descendents, including adoptive descendents, of the company founders. Nominations must be submitted to the Board Development Committee by April (or 3 months prior to annual shareholders' meeting).

3. The Board Development Committee makes the final decision on all board nominees. The CEO submits the list of nominees to the shareholders for consideration at the annual shareholders meeting.

4. The Family Council votes to elect new board members.

5. At this time, the Family Council recommends to the board of directors that family directors serve two-year terms, with an

annual evaluation completed by shareholders and an opportunity to end a term after one year. A family director may be considered for a second term, but may not serve more than two consecutive two-year terms. At least one year must elapse after two consecutive terms before a family director may be nominated again. Terms of each family director will be staggered with other family directors serving on the board.

Family Directors—Qualifications

The qualifications of family directors are different than those applied to independent directors. There is a need for capabilities that promote trust between the family shareholder group and the family director and board; trust that the family director is qualified to do the job. The following qualifications are those the Family Council will use to select family representatives to the board of directors:

Family Sensitivity and Communication Skills

Family directors should possess an ability to clearly articulate concepts and events, and an intuitive understanding of timing and frequency of communication to maximize trust and confidence. This requires a special sensitivity to the nature of the family and family dynamics, and knowledge of family issues and idiosyncrasies. The family director should be a good listener and should be open to the concerns or ideas expressed by other family members. The family director should have the ability to communicate in a respectful manner with all family members.

Diplomatic Dissention Skills

Family directors should possess an ability to assertively disagree with enough forcefulness to be heard, without attacking, such that one's comments promote an engaging exchange of views as opposed to defensiveness and counterattacking. The family director should be assertive, but also be a team player. The family director should have the courage and willingness to speak one's mind, while also possessing the diplomatic skills needed to avoid the potential for family conflict in front of nonfamily members.

Business Understanding and Acumen

Family directors should have prior experience in exercising sound business judgment, a basic knowledge of the business' industry, competitors, clients, products, and services, the business model and company strategies along with a working understanding of the financial statements and key performance measures. Examples of basic expertise include:

- Understanding of balance sheets, including differences between current assets and fixed assets, differences between current and long-term liabilities, the various aspects of shareholders' equity (stock, paid in capital, retained earnings, etc.).
- Ability to read financial statements, with understanding of how operational or net profits are calculated, understanding of EBITDA.
- Basic understanding of financial ratios, such as current ratio, return on investment, return on equity, average collection days, discounted cash flow analysis.
- Specific, in-depth expertise of tax, legal, financial, real estate, international, or other operational experience may also qualify.
- Basic understanding of strategic and operational planning.

The family director should also be willing to learn aspects of business that are unclear or unknown. In addition, it is critical that family directors have a good grasp of the family business' culture, the family's values, and how they are expressed in the business. For family director candidates with no prior board experience, consideration should be given to taking a course on the role and responsibilities of a board member.

High Level of Integrity

Family director candidates shall have recognized integrity and be a trusted and respected member of the family. The family director must be able to maintain confidentiality.

Ability to Collaborate with Management

Family directors should bring an understanding of, and ability to manage, the boundary between board and management, such that a family director can participate in holding management accountable, yet maintain the discipline to not interfere in management activities, while participating as a team member with the CEO to collaboratively take on the most critical strategic challenges faced by the business. The family director should be inquisitive, but not intrusive, should be professional and harbor no personal agendas.

Represent Family Shareholders

Family directors should understand and be able to effectively carry out, the fiduciary responsibility a director has to all shareholders. The family director should have the savvy to know when to act on behalf of the shareholder group as their representative and when to communicate upcoming board agenda items in advance and gain sufficient input to allow for an informed position.

Good Judgment

Family directors should have a confidence-inspiring ability to formulate opinions that incorporate objective data when available, combined with an intuitive sense for what is appropriate for the family shareholder group, and how best to go about achieving it. The family director should be decisive.

Leadership and Special Experience

Family directors should have a proven record of accomplishment in a prior leadership position and other specific experience based on the needs of the business, such as scientific, financial, legal, marketing, or international knowledge. Ideally, the family director will be a strategic thinker.

Appendix 4

Introductory Letter to Accompany Prospectus

Dear Colleague,

The owners of XYZ Corporation are beginning a board development process. Over the past several months, our ownership group has been meeting to discuss opportunities to ensure the successful transition of the business from the current generation to the next. As part of those efforts, we have determined that we would be well served to create a board composed of owners and independent directors who can provide support and counsel to management and owners.

We know that the success of this effort will be dependent upon identifying independent directors who appreciate our family business culture and values, understand the role of the independent directors and bring the skills and expertise we need to move our business forward. Jim Doe, who has been acquainted with our family for a number of years, suggested you might be a good candidate for our board.

We hope that you might consider being a candidate for a director position. We have enclosed a board prospectus that provides information on the company, position responsibilities, and the desired profile for directors. We will be in touch next week to see if you would like to participate in the interview process.

Sincerely,
John Smith
Chair, Nominating Committee (and second-generation owner)
XYZ Corporation

Appendix 5

Rating Sheet to Aid in Director Selection Meeting

Candidate evaluation

Rank as 3 (exceeds), 2 (meets), or 1 (does not meet)

Similar experience	Jim	John	Ann	Susan	Jeff
2nd to 3rd generation ownership transition					
Expanding through acquisition					
Concentrated customer base					
Management experience in similar size business					
Other relevant areas of experience					
Strategic planning					
Building a brand					
Building strong management team					
Governance experience					
Consensus building					
Conflict resolution					
For-profit board experience					
Personality					
Action oriented/problem solving					
Easy to get along with					
Creative					
Open to new ideas					
Total					

Appendix 6

Board of Directors Evaluation

The purpose of this evaluation is to provide a basis for evaluating the effectiveness of the board and how well it is meeting its objectives. Please consider all questions and mark only one answer for each, adding comments in the box to explain your response as appropriate.

	Not adequately	Adequately	To a great extent

1. **Board role**
   - Are the role and responsibilities of the board clearly defined and understood?
   - Does the board monitor corporate planning, budgeting and operations?
   - Does the board ensure adequate strategic plan development and implementation?
   - Does the board ensure succession plans are in place at a senior management level?

2. **Shareholder relations**
   - How well have the shareholders' objectives and expectations been communicated to the board?
   - Is there full and accurate reporting on Company affairs to the shareholders?

- Do independent board members have an adequate opportunity to develop a relationship with shareholders?

3. **Company strategy and direction**
   - Is the level of strategic planning carried out of sufficient quality and content to provide clear strategic direction for the Company?
   - Does the board dedicate adequate time to identifying, analyzing, and discussing strategic issues?
   - Does the board review the Company's performance against the strategic plan?

4. **Risk management**
   - Does the board adequately identify risks facing the company?
   - Does the board have a plan to address risks faced by the business?

5. **CEO support and oversight**
   - How clearly is the CEO's job description defined?
   - Is the CEO satisfactorily supported by appropriate counsel from the board?
   - Is the CEO's performance monitored and appraised satisfactorily?
   - Does the board have adequate access to key management?

6. **Board meetings**
   - Does the board receive the appropriate information to fulfill its governance responsibilities?
   - Are the frequency and style of board meetings appropriate?
   - Is the duration of board meetings appropriate?
   - Does the board agenda accurately reflect the key strategic issues facing the business?

7. **Board culture**
   - Does the board debate topics effectively, with all directors expressing their opinions?
   - Is balanced participation encouraged across all directors?
   - Is there recognition and use of individual board members' particular skills?
   - Are issues raised in the boardroom adequately captured, addressed, and resolved?
8. **Board composition and structure**
   - Is the size of the board appropriate?
   - Does the board have the appropriate mix of shareholders, management, and independent directors?
   - Does the committee structure support board decision making?
   - Is there a clear process for identifying needs on the board and finding directors to fill those needs?

What have been the board's greatest contributions over the past year?

What areas could the board improve upon in the coming year?

What should the board's priorities be over the next year?

Appendix 7

Chairman Job Description

I. Basic Function

The chairman of the board serves as the board's agent retained for the proper execution of corporate governance functions. As such, the chairman organizes and manages the functioning of the board itself, such that the Company's total activities are aligned with Company values, mission, and strategic objectives as well as laws applying to the activities of the firm. Further, the chairman provides specified liaison, relationship enhancement, and development activities between the board and outsiders, which are strategic in supporting the long-term health and growth of the Company.

II. Responsibility and Authority

A. Policy
  1. Formulates board policy proposals concerning reserved board powers, the proper functioning of the board and its committees, and places such proposals on board agenda for action.
  2. Reviews with the CEO Company policies, plans, budgets, and the like, to assist in preparation for presentation to the board.
B. Shareholder Relations
  1. Maintains and directs shareholder relations so that shareholders' confidence in the Company is strengthened and their values pursued.
  2. Prepares calls for shareholder meetings, with assistance of other corporate officers, and signs official communications to the shareholders.

3. Prepares the agenda for shareholders' meetings and presides over meetings.

4. Ensures that the shareholders are properly informed about the financial condition, the opportunities, and risks to the Company and receives counsel as appropriate from the shareholders.

C. Family Council Relations

1. Serves as the primary communications link between the Family Council and the board of directors.

2. Actively represents the views of the Family Council at board meetings.

3. Identifies issues at the board level for input from the Family Council.

D. The Board of Directors

1. Prepares for timely distribution board meeting agendas, advance information packages, and such other information as may properly flow to the board.

2. Oversees the development and implementation of board-evaluation processes. Reviews evaluation results and recommends remedies to the board.

3. Facilitates obtaining adequate response to requests for information from other directors.

4. Guides the board in discharging its responsibilities, drawing from directors their maximum contributions, and assisting in the resolution of any differences that may arise among them.

5. Performs other duties, as assigned by the board or by committees of the board.

6. Reviews management proposals, reports, presentations, and recommendations that will be made to the board and assigns them to the appropriate committee or the general board for action.

7. Coordinates with the CEO the implementation of board decisions to ensure their effectiveness.

8. Councils the CEO in the preparation of reports and proposals for submission to the board or its committees.

E. The Board Meeting

1. Presides at all board meetings and serves as a voting member of the board.

2. Proposes time and place of board meetings, including special meetings.

    3. Directs the board toward policy matters and away from involvement in operations.

F. Committees of the Board

    1. Identifies the needs for creating or dissolving board committees, including definition of powers, and makes recommendations to the board for action.

    2. Appoints committee members and chairpersons, subject to board approval.

    3. Works with the committee chairmen and the CEO to ensure the effective functioning of the board and its committees.

    4. Serves as an ex-officio nonvoting member of all committees.

G. Planning

    1. Ensures that a short-range and long-range business planning process is in place and remains actively involved in establishing objectives, defining strategy, and identifying associated implementation steps.

    2. Ensures that the board regularly evaluates management performance against the strategic plans and holds management accountable to the plan.

H. Special Strategic Responsibilities

    1. Represents the Company in relations with the government to identify, promote, and establish corporate interests.

    2. Represents the company in relations with the local and global community in order to develop and promote common interests.

    3. Administers the Company contributions program, as adopted by the board, and approves all donations.

Appendix 8

Smith[1] Family Assembly Charter

Preamble

Recognizing the need for an organized network to promote family interaction, communication, and education among members of the four branches of the John Smith, Sr., family and our collectively owned companies, we, the descendents of John Smith, Sr., hereby set forth this Charter establishing a Smith Family Assembly and Family Council.

Mission

We make this statement as part of our shared goal of being good stewards of our family and its businesses:

We aspire to the following ideals:

Accountability
Amicability
Appropriate engagement in our family businesses
Balance
Education about our businesses and otherwise
Effective, open, and structured communication
Empathy
Fairness
Family Unity
Forgiveness

---

[1] Fictitious name

Growing our companies so that they provide competitive returns
for all stakeholders
Leadership succession planning
Maintaining qualified independent boards of directors
Minimizing conflicts of interest
Planning
Philanthropy
Positivity
Resolving disputes
Sustainability
Transparency of purpose and action

As stakeholders in our family businesses, we are committed to practicing these principles to help ensure their future success and stability. We want to do our part to increase their value to our customers, vendors, employees, stockholders and communities.

Ultimately, we wish to build on the investments and efforts of previous generations in order for our companies to continue as successful family businesses for the benefit of subsequent generations.

Purpose of Family Assembly and Council

The Family Assembly and Council are dedicated to cultivating the legacy of the descendents of John Smith, Sr.

The goals of the Family Assembly are to create social events, educate family members about the family businesses, facilitate relations between these family-owned businesses and the extended family, and ensure that future generations of the John Smith family will have a sense of enduring pride in their family legacy.

The Family Council shall be the administrative board for the Family Assembly.

Family Assembly

Membership

All adult descendents of John Smith, Sr., are considered to be Family Assembly members and are encouraged to participate in the Assembly. Family Assembly membership shall also include:

- Spouses of Family members
- Spouses of deceased Family members
- Individuals legally adopted into our Family.

Member Rights and Responsibilities

1. Sustain and enhance the Family.
2. Strive to fulfill the Family Assembly Mission.
3. Participate in the Family Assembly.
4. Volunteer for service in the Family Assembly and Council.
5. Elect the Family Council and committee chairmen.
6. Approve and amend this Family Assembly Charter.
7. Vote on matters brought before the Assembly.
8. Make recommendations to the Family Council.
9. Participate in Family Council meetings at the discretion of the Council chairman.

Family Assembly Meetings

1. There shall be an annual meeting of the Family Assembly at a date and time to be determined by the Family Council.
2. The Family Assembly shall hold elections for all Council positions and committee chairs every 2 years at its annual meeting.
3. Any group of at least 5 Assembly members or the Council may call an Assembly meeting.
4. Due process for calling a meeting of the Family Assembly shall entail providing at least 15 days advance written notice, sent to all Assembly members using their most recently provided contact information. The notice shall include the purpose for calling the meeting as well as documentation of major proposals to be presented at that meeting.
5. Parents may allow their children 14 or older whom they deem mature enough to understand the proceedings to observe Family Assembly meetings.
6. Observer participation in Assembly meetings shall be at the discretion of the Council chairman.
7. Meeting procedures shall follow the current edition of Robert's Rules of Order.

Assembly Voting

1. Each Assembly member 18 years of age or older may vote on Council elections and actions brought by the Council to the whole Assembly.
2. All Assembly members' votes shall be counted equally.
3. A quorum shall be met when 10 or more Family Assembly members cast votes on any issue.
4. Election voting shall be held by secret ballot.
5. A simple majority of all votes cast shall determine the outcome of elections and actions.
6. The Family Council may bring certain matters before the Assembly for discussion and voting.
7. One or more tellers will be appointed by the secretary of the Council to tally votes.
8. Votes may be cast in person, electronically to the secretary and/or chairman of the Family Council or by proxy signed over to another Family Assembly member. If anyone votes by more than one method, the most recent shall prevail.
9. A quorum of the Family Assembly has the right to call for a vote at a properly convened meeting to override a decision of the Family Council and committees.

Family Council

Membership

1. Family Assembly members 19 years of age and older are eligible to be Council members.
2. With the goal that all eligible Family Assembly members be involved in some way with the Family Council, Assembly members who have not previously held positions on the Council are encouraged to volunteer.
3. Family Council members are the officers, committee chairmen and co-chairmen directly elected by the Family Assembly, except as provided for replacement members in this Charter.
4. Council and committee members who are not stockholders in the Company may not hold a position directly pertaining to that Company.

Nominations to the Family Council

1. The presiding Family Council chairman shall appoint a nominating committee of at least three people to propose a slate of candidates for the succeeding term of Family Council officers and committee chairmen.
2. Nominations may also be provided from the floor prior to election voting.
3. All Family Council candidates must consent to serving prior to being added to the ballot.
4. All nominees must be elected by the Family Assembly in order to be affirmed as officers of the Family Council and committee chairmen.

Family Council Meetings

1. Family Council meetings shall be held at least twice a year or more often if deemed necessary to conduct Council business.
2. In order to ensure transparency, Family Council meetings are open to any Family Assembly members who would like to observe them. Occasionally, discussion of business matters may be open only to stockholders, as determined by the Council chairman.
3. Parents may allow their children 14 or older whom they deem mature enough to understand the proceedings to observe Family Council meetings.
4. Observer participation in Council meetings shall be at the discretion of the Council chairman.
5. Meeting procedures shall follow the current edition of Robert's Rules of Order.

Council Structure

1. A Family Council chairman shall be elected by the Family Assembly to fulfill the following responsibilities:
   a. Lead the Family Council and ensure its performance.
   b. Moderate discussions among the Council and during Assembly meetings.

    c. When appropriate, attend family businesses' boards of directors meetings as the liaison from the Family Assembly and Council. If the Council chairman is not a stockholder of a specific family business, she or he may appoint someone who is a stockholding Family Assembly member of that business as liaison to its board of directors.

2. A Family Council vice-chairman shall be elected by the Family Assembly to fulfill the following responsibilities:

    a. Assist the Council chairman in his or her duties and act in the chairman's stead when this individual is not able to attend meetings.

    b. Serve as chairman of the Charter Committee and advise the Family Council and Assembly on questions regarding application of the provisions of, and amendments to, the John Smith Family Charter.

    c. The goal shall be to elect a vice chairman of a generation different from that of the chairman.

3. When willing and able participants can be found, two representatives from each of the four branches of the Smith Family (Joan, John, Jr., James, and Mary) shall be elected to the Family Council. The goal shall be to elect an adult representative from each generation of the Family Assembly to the Council leadership and committees.

    a. In addition to the officers and committee chairmen, at-large positions on the Family Council may be elected to help meet this goal.

    b. Eligible at-large positions will be determined after tallying the election results of the other Family Council officers and committee chairmen. At-large positions shall be offered only to persons who would fulfill the missing family branch and generational representation goals of the Council as outlined above.

    c. Immediately following vote tallying for Family Council positions at the same Family Assembly meeting, if needed, an election shall be held to attempt to fill eligible at-large Family Council positions.

4. An officer or chairman may serve multiple roles.

5. The number of Family Council members shall be odd, and between 7 and 13 in number.

6. By simple majority vote, the Family Council may elect an interim replacement Council member to fill a vacant Council office or committee chair.
   a. This replacement Council member shall serve until a special election can be held to fill the position at the next Family Assembly meeting.
   b. This replacement Council member shall have Family Council member voting privileges for the duration of this interim service.

Committee Structure

1. Each Family Council member shall serve as the chairman, co-chairman or member of a standing committee.
   a. Each committee chairman may invite as many Family Assembly members to join his/her committee as necessary to conduct the business of that committee.
   b. These invited committee members are not necessarily members of the Family Council.
2. The Family Council may create as many additional committees as needed to conduct the business of the Council.
   a. The Family Council will appoint an interim chairman to organize a new committee and serve as its chairman until the next Family Assembly meeting.
   b. At that Assembly meeting a special election will be held for the chairmanship of the recently formed committee to serve until the next regular election.

Terms for Officers and Committee Chairs

1. Elections for all Family Council members shall be held every two years at the Family Assembly meetings.
2. Terms for officers and committee chairmen shall be two years.
3. Special elections may result in terms of less than two years in the following circumstances:
   a. the first elected term for the chairman of a recently formed committee;
   b. an officer or committee chairman elected to fill a vacancy.

4. If re-elected, an officer or committee chairman may serve for two consecutive terms. If there is no other candidate to fill a position, the person holding that position may continue after 2 terms until a new officer or committee chairman is elected.

5. A Council member may be re-elected after sitting off the Council for one term.

Council and Committee Voting Procedures

1. The Family Assembly voting procedures shall also apply to the Family Council and committees except as specified in this Charter.

2. For all voting, each Council member shall have one vote, regardless of a member holding multiple Council positions.

3. A Council quorum shall be a simple majority of all Council members.

4. Only Family Council members shall have Family Council voting authority.

5. A committee quorum shall be a simple majority of its members.

6. Elected and appointed committee members may vote on matters in front of their respective committee.

7. A quorum of Council members may overrule a decision made by the Family Council chairman or a standing committee.

Standing Committees

Standing committees shall be permanent components of the Family Assembly and Council. Within the bounds of each committee's respective scope, its purpose shall be helping accomplish the Family Assembly's goals. At annual Family Assembly meetings, each standing committee chairman shall report on the activities of that committee during the prior year.

Charter Committee

The Charter Committee shall recommend and facilitate necessary amendments to this Charter. Any proposed amendment to this Charter must be sent to all Family Assembly members 15 days prior to the meeting at which the amendment is to be presented.

Communications Committee

The Communications Committee shall facilitate Family Assembly and Council communication to and from all family members, including use of the family website. This committee shall also be responsible for maintaining a current email, phone, and mailing address list for all family members, active and inactive. If a member of the family wishes to send a message to the Family Assembly at large, it may be sent to the Communications chairman, who shall forward it to everyone else. This person shall serve as secretary of the Family Council and send updates on pertinent Council matters to Family Assembly members.

Education Committee

The Education Committee will provide age-appropriate educational programs for Smith family children and adults. Topics could include family history, company history, information about the businesses, and what it means to be a stockholder. This committee would also coordinate tours of family-owned businesses once or twice a year.

Finance Committee

The Finance Committee shall arrange programs and seminars for family members on financial and estate planning, and present ways the family's personal wealth and company assets can work together. The chairman of this committee will serve as treasurer of the Family Council. The treasurer shall work with other Council members to collect and allocate funds for activities pertaining to Family Assembly and Council matters. The treasurer shall provide an annual financial report to the Assembly. Assembly and Council financial records shall be made available upon request to Assembly members throughout the year.

Historical Archive Committee

The Historical Archive Committee shall collect and record the family's and its companies' histories. It will also organize documents and pictures into one or more formats which will be made available for family access.

Philanthropy Committee

We believe it is the duty, obligation, and privilege of our family to give back to the community. Contributions should reflect Smith family values while keeping in mind the strategic needs of our companies. The purpose of the Philanthropy Committee is to ensure that our longstanding tradition of philanthropy continues.

The family-owned companies' boards of directors shall determine the amount of money available for philanthropic donation on an annual basis. The Philanthropy Committee shall include at least one member from the Family Assembly at large, as well as two stockholders, a director of the board and a manager from each company potentially offering financial contributions to the funds available for philanthropic purposes. The committee shall communicate with the family and companies to determine the values and priorities to direct corporate donations within the community and oversee the distribution of gifts.

Social Committee

The Social Committee of the Smith Family Assembly has the goal of providing the opportunity for enjoyable recreational and social interaction twice a year. We strive to invite all family members for at least two events per year. We will coordinate the food and the recreational equipment within an appropriate budget based on past events. We will report the results of the events for family members who could not attend. It is our ultimate goal to develop good memories and close relationships within our extended family.

Summary of Survey Results

Family Business Boards Survey Summary

Demographics

Who Was Part of Our Research Sample?

360 valid survey responses were collected from electronic surveys among members of the Young President's Organization, readers of the *Family Business Advisor* (a monthly subscription newsletter covering family business issues), and members of university-based family business centers.

48% have a functional board, defined as a board the meets at least three times per year

All remaining statistics reported are based on the subset of the total sample that indicated that they had a "Functional Board."

Size of Businesses by Revenues[a]	
Less than $10 Million	13%
$10–$25 Million	15%
$26–$50 Million	15%
$51–$100 Million	17%
$101–$250 Million	15%
Over $251 Million	24%

Youngest Generation of Ownership[a]

1st Generation (founders)	9%
2nd Generation	32%
3rd Generation	26%
4th Generation	19%
5th Generation or more	13%

Total Number of Owners in Business[a]

1	2%
2 to 5	45%
6 to 10	14%
11 or more	40%

Ownership of Shares Held Outside Family

100% Family Owned	66%
Family less than 100% but 51% or more	26%
Nonfamily owns 50% or more of shares	6%

Board Composition

Boards by Type

Family Board	75%
2 or more Independents	25%
3 or more Independents	21%
Majority Independent	16%

Percentage of Given Board Type by Revenue Split[b]

	Less than $10 Million	$10–$25 Million	$26–$50 Million	$51–$100 Million	$101–$250 Million	Over $251 Million
Family Board	94%	95%	62%	54%	52%	40%
2 or More Independents	0%	5%	19%	21%	24%	23%
Majority Independents	6%	0%	19%	25%	24%	37%

Ownership representation on the Board

All owners sit on board	39%
All owners do NOT sit on board	61%
Nonemployed owners on board	40%

Size of Board (number of directors)

3	4	5	6	7	8	9
14%	12%	17%	14%	11%	13%	20%

Leadership, Structure, Policies & Process

Leadership

CEO is a family member	85%
CEO and Chair are same person	63%

Number of board meetings held per year

2–3	4–5	6–7	8 or more
25%	49%	10%	16%

Total Number of Committees Reported

0	1	2	3	4
66%	5%	14%	10%	5%

Percentage of Respondents with Forced Retirement Mechanisms

Term limits	6%
Mandatory retirement age	11%

Percentage of Respondents with Board Preparation/Evaluation processes

Process in place to prepare family for board service	12%
Have conducted a board evaluation	18%

Compensation Structure

No compensation	42%
Annual retainer	32%
Per meeting fees	44%
Retainer & meeting fees	18%
Stock options	4%
Other incentive compensation	4%

Board Value

Percentage of Respondents Who Rated Their Board Effective in Ensuring the Business Is Well Managed

	Overall Average	Family Board	2 or more Independents	Majority Independents
Not Effective	9%	11%	4%	3%
Marginally Effective	25%	35%	13%	0%
Effective	46%	37%	70%	55%
Highly Effective	21%	17%	13%	41%

Value provided by board (Average of All Respondents on a Scale Of 1-5, with 5 Representing Significant Contribution, 1 Representing No Contribution)

	Overall Average	Family Board	2 or more Independents	Majority Independents
Help with Strategic Direction	4.05	3.78	3.96	4.38
Sounding board for Management	3.91	3.67	3.78	4.24
Help ensure owners goals considered	3.73	3.71	3.70	3.76
Functional expertise	3.63	3.57	3.65	3.66
Help with objectivity	3.67	3.59	3.69	3.72
Enforce follow-through on plans	3.63	3.39	3.48	4.00
Help with succession	3.46	3.3	3.17	3.86
Industry Expertise	3.06	2.75	3.35	3.14
Network	2.72	2.46	2.78	2.90

In this appendix, the figures are based on respondents who answered the question. Sample varies slightly by question.

Notes

a These figures are reported for the respondents who have active boards (48% of the sample)

b Numbers represent the percentage of businesses in a particular revenue category that have a particular board make-up (e.g., of businesses with revenues less than $10 million, 94% have a family board)

Bibliography

ABA, *Model Business Corporation Act*
3rd edition, Adopted by the Committee on Corporate Laws of the Section of Business Law with support of the American Bar Foundation. 2003. http://www.abanet.org/buslaw/library/onlinepublications/mbca2002.pdf.

Corporate Directors Guidebook, 5th edition, Committee on Corporate Laws American Bar Association. August 2007.

Coutts and Co. "Coutts 2005 Family Business Survey." London: 2005. http://www.finh.com/cmsAdmin/uploads/045_05_08_2010_Coutts_Family_Business_Survey_001.pdf.

Laird Norton Tyee. "Laird Norton Tyee Family Business Survey Family to Family." Seattle, Washington: 2007. http://familybusinesssurvey.com/2007/pdfs/LNT_FamilyBusinessSurvey_2007.pdf.

National Association of Corporate Directors. "When Good Boards Don't Work." *Director's Monthly*, August, 2000.

Price Waterhouse Cooper. "Making a Difference: The Price Waterhouse Cooper's Family Business Survey 2007/2008." 2007. http://www.pwc.com/pt_BR/br/estudos-pesquisas/assets/making-difference.pdf.

Tillinghast, Towers Perrin. "2005 Directors and Officers Liability Survey." Chicago: 2005. http://www.towersperrin.com/tillinghast/publications/reports/2005_DO/DO_2005_Exec_Sum.pdf.

Ward, U.L, and Handy, J.L "Survey of Board Practices." *Family Business Review*, 1988, *1 (3)*, 289–308.

Index

academics, as director
candidates, 92
accountability, 17–18, 23, 32, 42,
52, 67–69, 74, 76, 112, 184,
212, 214
active boards
audit committees and, 83
board member selection and,
70–71
CEOs and, 26
committees, 83, 137
conflict and, 12
oversight and accountability, 68
risk profile and, 64
terms of service, 81–82
value of, 2–3, 4, 7, 35
advice, offering, 200
age, search for directors
and, 99
approaching candidates, 103–6
audit committee
responsibilities, 222
sample charter, 223–25

benefits of boards
challenging, provocative
questions, 20–21
confidential and empathetic
counsel, 21
creative thinking and decision
making, 21–22

honest, objective opinions,
18–19
in-house experience, 17
insight into key people, 19–20
self-discipline and
accountability, 17–18
sounding board, 18
strategic planning and
counsel, 19
valuable corporate relations,
22–23
board background book, 128–32
board experience
CEOs and, 101
directors and, 101–2
board input, dealing with
avoid over-explaining, 150
decision making, 151
feedback, 151
listening, 150
patience, 151
sense of humor, 151
board of directors
example evaluation, 233–35
example prospectus, 217–21
boardroom culture, 174–75,
179–80
boards of directors, independent
benefits of, 17–23
fears and misconceptions
about, 13–17

boards of directors—*Continued*
  fundamentals of, 28–34
  importance in family business,
    3–4
  legal role, 27–28
  overview, 1–3
  resistance to, 11–13
  as symbol of continuity and
    dedication, 51–52
  when to use, 4–7
boards, structure of
  committees, 82–83
  terms of service, 81–82
breakthrough thinking, 147–51
bureaucracy, 13, 16–17
business continuity planning
  achievability, 60–61
  ensuring validity of plan,
    58–59
  estate plan, 56
  evaluation strategic planning
    process, 59
  family continuity plan, 56–57
  overseeing plan development, 58
  overview, 53–54
  sound information, 59–61
  strategic plan, 54–55
  strategic thinking, 61–66
  succession plan, 55–56

Canal Insurance, 67–68, 89, 95, 183
candidates for directorship
  academics, 92
  division heads, 92–93
  friends, 90–91
  other CEOs, entrepreneurs,
    and business owners, 93–94
  paid advisers, 90
  people holding multiple
    directorships, 92
  retirees, 91–92

candidness, 190–91
CEOs
  board input and, 150–51
  board leadership and, 118–20
  board support for, 26, 28,
    49–50, 66
  compensation, 86, 181–82
  competing roles, 48–49
  cooperation with board, 190
  corporate mission statement
    and, 30
  cost of capital and, 62–63
  creative thinking and, 22,
    147–48
  as director candidates, 93–94
  financial matters and, 46–47
  independent directors and,
    10–11, 18
  lack of board experience and,
    101
  meetings and, 120, 123, 126
  openness and, 149
  organizational culture and,
    33–34
  performance vs. potential,
    61–62
  prospectus development and,
    76
  record-keeping and, 134–35
  risk profile and, 64
  stakeholder interests and,
    28–30
  strategic planning and, 58–59
  succession planning and, 38,
    40, 42–45, 48
chairman, job description
  basic function, 236
  responsibility and authority,
    236–38
Collat, Charles Sr., 53
committees

forming and managing, 137–38
increasing board effectiveness
  with, 156–57
overview, 82–83
compensation committee
explained, 138
responsibilities, 222–23
sample charter, 224–25
compensation
board and, 176, 186–87
directors and, 86–88
competing roles, balancing,
  48–49
competition, in boardroom, 202
conflicts, avoiding, 146
contingency plans, 64–65, 196
control, 13–14
conversations, managing, 147
corporate mission statements,
  30–31
corporate values statements,
  31–32
cost of capital, 62–63
creativity, leadership and, 153–55
culture, search for directors and,
  99–100

Danco, Leon, 93
decisions, deferment of, 199
designing boards
board profile, 77
choosing members, 68–72
compensation for directors,
  86–88
director's personal qualities,
  80–81
future direction, 78–79
future growth, 78
industry profile, 77–78
keys to success, 78
overview, 67–68

owners' long-term aspirations
  and, 79–80
prospectus, 74–77
role of independent directors
  in structure, 72–74
scheduling meetings, 84–86
sources of future growth, 78
structure of board, 81–83
transition period, 83–84
directors, contributing as
asking effective questions,
  193–97
factors to consider before
  serving, 189–93
resources for all directors,
  208–9
showing interest in business,
  197–98
special issues for directors of
  family-owned business,
  203–7
supporting CEO and chair,
  198–203
supporting succession and
  family employee
  development, 207
unique roles for family
  directors, 207–8
directors, finding and selecting
aim high, 94–95
approaching candidates, 103–6
beginning search, 89–94
case study, 113–16
cross-checking candidates, 108
dealing with fears of rejection
  or mistakes, 102–3
dealing with mistakes, 111–12
director liability, 106–8
how to say no, 110–11
how to search, 97–98
making final selections, 108–10

directors,—*Continued*
overview, 89
participants in search, 95–97
sample rating sheet, 232
subtleties of search, 98–102
directors, independent
family education, 50–61
help with ongoing business
issues, 46–49
overview, 35–37
planning for orderly
management succession,
37–46
stabilizing influence for family,
49–50
disclosure, 15, 23, 136, 182, 224
division heads, as director
candidates, 92–93

empathy, 200–1
entrepreneurial plateaus, 5
estate plans, 56
evaluating board, 141–44
expertise, directors and, 77, 100–1

family and business governance
board compensation, 186–87
board interface with
shareholders, 180–82
board selection process, 176–79
board structure, 182–84
boardroom culture, 179–80
choosing appropriate structure,
170–73
establishing, 170
evolution of, 166–70
family director effectiveness,
184–85
topics important to, 172–73
tricky issues in governance,
174–76

family assemblies, sample charter,
239–48
family business boards, survey
summary
board composition, 250–51
board value, 252
demographics, 249–50
leadership, structure, policies,
and process, 251
family continuity plans, 56–57
family councils
establishing, 170
role of, 171–73
family directors
business understanding and
acumen, 229–30
collaboration with
management, 230
diplomatic dissention skills,
228–29
effectiveness, 175, 184–85
good judgment, 230
integrity, 229
leadership and special
experience, 230
nomination process, 227–28
qualifications, 228–29
representing family
shareholders, 230
sensitivity and communication
skills, 228
family education, 50–51
fears and misconceptions about
boards, 13–17
being forced to act too
quickly, 16
bureaucracy, 16–17
difficulty in choosing, 15
liability risks, 14–15
loss of control, 13–14
not organized, 15–16

outsiders, 16
privacy, 15
respect for values, 14
final selections, 108–10
financial matters, 46–47
friends, as director candidates,
90–91
Fully Leveraged Boards, 123,
125–26
future growth, ownership profile
and, 78–79

gender, search for directors and,
99–100
Goedecke, Nancy, 53
governance committee, 111–12,
114, 138, 142, 183, 223

habitual thinking, 195–96

inappropriate choices, 111–12
independent directors
see directors, independent
industry profile, 77

legal role of boards, 27–28
liability risks, 14–15, 106–8
long-term aspirations, 79–80

management succession, board
and, 37–46
aid in timely succession
planning, 38–39
examining options, 39–40
helping with organizational
succession, 45–46
monitoring final stages, 43–45
planning for process, 40–41
preparing for successor, 41–43
as safety net, 38
managing boards

advance planning, 120–28
between-meeting
communications, 140–41
board background book,
128–32
choosing chair, 118–20
organizing new board, 133–39
evaluating and changing
board, 141–44
overview, 117–18
preparing advance meeting
materials, 133
running first meeting, 139–40
Mathile, Clayton, 149, 191
Mayer Electric Supply, 53
McKee Foods Corp., 32–33,
67–68, 117
meaningful input, board
structure and, 191
meetings
between-meeting
communications, 140–41
initial, 139–40
invitees, 127–28
location, 120–21
number of, 84–85
preparing agendas, 122–27
preparing materials, 133
schedule and topics, 121–22
structure, 85–86
minutes, keeping, 136
Model Business Corporations Act
(MBCA), 27

National Association of
Corporate Directors
(NACD), 26, 73, 85, 87,
97, 208
next-generation evaluation,
47–48
nondisclosure agreements, 105

openness, 149–50
optimizing boards
  committees, 156–57
  creating appropriate board
    culture, 152–53
  creativity through leadership,
    153–55
  facilitating breakthrough
    thinking, 147–51
  managing boardroom,
    146–47
  overview, 145–46
  special uses for independent
    directors, 160–63
  troubleshooting, 157–60
organizational culture, assessing,
  32–34
organizational succession, 45–46
outsiders, fear of, 16
ownership profile, 78–79

paid advisers, as director
  candidates, 90
personal qualities, 80–81
Plato, 28
privacy, 15
prospectus
  contents of, 75
  overview, 74–76
  sample introductory letter to
    accompany, 231

quorums, 133–34

rejection, fear of, 102–3
resistance to boards, 12–14
resolutions, 136–37
retirees, as director candidates,
  91–92
risk profile, 64
Rodale (company), 1–2, 55

Rodale, Maria, 1
Rodale, Robert, 1

Schurz Communications,
  113–16
search process for directors
  candidates, 89–94
  identifying candidates, 97–98
  participants in process, 95–96
  setting standards, 94–95
  subtleties of, 98–102
secretaries, 134–35
selection/election of boards,
  174
shareholders, board interface
  with, 175, 180–82
stakeholder interests, 28–30
strategic planning
  ensuring achievability, 60–61
  ensuring validity of, 58–59
  evaluating process, 59
  overseeing of plan
    development, 58
  overview, 54–55
  questions to ask, 59–60
  role of directors in, 57–58
strategic profile, 77–78
strategic thinking
  contingency plans, 64–65
  cost of capital, 62–63
  growth vs. good return, 62
  human-resources planning,
    65–66
  maximizing value of business,
    63–64
  performance vs. potential,
    61–62
  risk profile of business, 64
strengths, playing to, 146
success, keys to, 78
succession

see management succession,
 board and; organizational
 succession
succession plans, 55–56

term limits, 81–82, 251
transition periods, 83–84
transparency, 17, 40, 178–79,
 212, 216

troubleshooting
 contested board, 159–60
 inflexible board members,
 158–59
 lack of follow-up, 160
 unimaginative agenda, 157–58

value-added chain, 128, 131, 203
values, 14

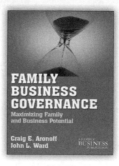
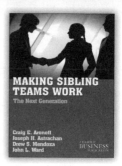

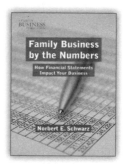
"Each Family Business Leadership publication is packed cover-to-cover with expert guidance, solid information and ideas that work."

—Alan Campbell, CFO, Campbell Motel Properties, Inc., Brea, CA

"While each volume contains helpful 'solutions' to the issues it covers, it is the guidance on how to tackle the process of addressing the different issues, and the emphasis on the benefits which can stem from the process itself, which make the Family Business publications of unique value to everyone involved in a family business—not just the owners."

—David Grant, Director (retired), William Grant & Sons Ltd. (distillers of Glenfiddich and other fine Scotch whiskeys)